# Dogs Ride

# Motorcycle Side Car Riding for Dogs (and Humans)

Timothy O'Connor

&

Connie O'Connor

Copyright © 2012 Timothy and Connie O'Connor

All rights reserved.

ISBN-13: 978-1502388612
ISBN-10: 1502388618

# DEDICATION

To Bourbon, whose desire to "work" inspired us to put him in a sidecar, and to Harley, who proved that an old dog *can* learn new tricks.

# CONTENTS

Acknowledgments

1 Why Sidecar Dogs?

2 Dog Training

3 Sidecar Outfitting

4 Choosing a Rig

5 Choosing the Mule

6 Choosing a Hack

7 Driver Training

8 Events, Giving Back

9 Resources

10 Credits, Sources

# ACKNOWLEDGMENTS

Dan at DBear Sidecar Works
Floyd Byrd
Kevin Combs
League for Animal Welfare, Batavia Ohio
All About Dogs, Cincinnati Ohio
Sheltered Paws Animal Rescue, Cincinnati Ohio
Ben at SideCar Pro
Tim Kaelin & Jay Eakins
Rick Markle
Cincinnati Street Style

# 1 WHY SIDECAR DOGS?

Every dog owner knows the feeling: that sense of guilt as you grab your keys and see your dog looking sullen at the doorway. Dogs are pack animals, and their humans are often the only pack they have. They evolved to be social creatures and to read human cues. Most often a dog's entire world revolves around his human family. Dogs seem to feel disappointed when we leave them behind and that might make us feel a little sad too.

If you love riding motorcycles you don't need to leave your four-legged friend behind. Motorcyclists know that riding can transform a ho-hum day into something special. While riding we are fully present, immersed in sights, sounds, smells, and sensations that we miss in an enclosed vehicle. For many, riding is a form of mindfulness, a meditation in the "now".

Kevin Johnson's dog Charlie doesn't want to be left at home.
(used with permission)

Now imagine riding with your dog – a friend who lives in the moment and experiences the world with a terrific sense of smell and hearing. Picture your best friend grinning into the wind, savoring every sensation and inspiring you to do the same. No more guilt about enjoying a beautiful day while your dog sits home alone. You are flying down the road together, a pack on the move, hunting for experiences, and life is very, very good.

You may think your dog doesn't have what it takes to ride sidecar. Many people sell their dogs short, never giving them the opportunity to show their true capabilities. Dogs are highly adaptable and can be trained throughout their lives. If you think "my dog could never do this" you just might be surprised. The real question is "are you willing to be a strong pack leader, and to establish a bond of trust with your dog?" If so, the two of you can move mountains together and certainly can ride sidecars.

Brian Sennikoff's pack rides with him to the ends of the road in his Honda GL1100 with Champion sidecar. (used with permission)

Judging by the number of thumbs-ups, honks, waves, and big smiles we get when the four of us are riding sidecars, we know that there are many dog lovers out there. Who doesn't love seeing happy dogs and their humans? It is a wonderful thing to know that we are spreading smiles and joy.

We can't stress enough how important it is for all dog owners to be considerate so that we can have the privilege of taking our dogs with us. Clean up after them, put down blankets so they don't shed on the hotel's bedding, keep them on leash and don't let them run up to people, tell people if your dog does not like strangers or other dogs *before* they get too close, and in general have them under control and behaving like well-trained citizens at all times.

La Quinta Inn is a dog friendly hotel chain that can be a great help on long trips across the US.

We have discovered many fun destinations for our sidecar dogs. Several hotel chains including La Quinita allow dogs. We rent a houseboat at Dale Hollow in Kentucky each year that allows them too. And of course, there's camping and outdoor dining. If you would like to share some of your favorite dog friendly establishments, hotels or services please let us know by emailing or posting to the Facebook page for this book.

Brian Sennikoff's pack apparently assisting him with driving. Buster Brown, Betty Lou Cooter Belle, Donna Belle, Baby Belle and Isabelle Junior. (photo

Timothy and Connie O'Connor
used with permission)

# 2 DOG TRAINING

Note: For the sake of simplicity, we'll use the name "Fido" for our hypothetical dog, and use male pronouns when referring to dogs in general.

What kind of dog do you have? A mellow fellow who takes everything in stride, a working dog who wants to please, or perhaps an active dog who chases squirrels and pulls you down the street on your morning walk? All can be trained to ride sidecar, but the pleasure of their company is only as great as your dedication to being a consistent and trustworthy leader. Your dog depends on you to keep him safe, to explain the rules, and to keep things positive.

All dog training is really "people training." Dogs have evolved with humans for many thousands of years; they know how to read us. But we are responsible for making our expectations perfectly clear, and to try to read their body language as well.. Do you know what situations make your dog feel threated? Can you see with a glance that your dog is tense, preparing to lunge out of the sidecar or bite an approaching person? Can you catch your dog while he's still *thinking* about doing something wrong, and correct him before things go too far? If so, bravo! If not, you may have some work to do.

## The Basics

A well trained dog is a true joy. When we see people's dogs pulling them down the street and tangling them up in a flexileash, and we see those same people unleashing their dogs in places they shouldn't just because it's such a hassle to walk them, we feel sorry both for dog and owner. Who is in control ? How stressful for them and everyone around them. It's not too hard to teach a dog to heel with the right trainer. Dogs are more calm and enjoy their walk more, we believe, when there are boundaries and when they are attentive to their handers.

So teach your dog the basics …to heel on and off leash, to sit and stay and lie down, reliably come when called, "watch me" or "pay attention" and "leave it" for things he should avoid. A good rule of thumb is that your dog should "earn" his dinner, his ride in the sidecar, his entrance into the house, etc. Simply requiring a "sit" before tossing a ball or allowing him to jump on the couch is a way to remind him that you are in control. This is important when things get scary for him ….he needs to know he has a strong leader.

**Introduction to the Sidecar**

Some people have been successful in just putting their dog in the sidecar and taking off. We don't recommend this because you don't want to find out that your dog isn't as laid back or calm as you thought when you're moving at 40 mph on the open road. If your dog isn't the flexible and resilient kind, he might be so scared from his first experience that he won't be willing to get back in, or if he does, he might not enjoy it. As they say, you only get one chance to make a first impression. Make it a great one.

First, make sure the sidecar is appropriate for your dog – a sturdy grippable floorboard, not too small for your dog, a place to tie into the harness, etc. Put the harness on your dog and heel him to the sidecar rig, which should be parked and off. When he sniffs it, praise and reward him with treats or affection. Even if he only glances at the sidecar, praise and reward. In a few repetitions, he will be pretty curious about this happy machine.

Give your dog a command to get into the sidecar, and assist him if needed. Keep in mind that even if a dog is willing to jump into the sidecar, he may hurt himself if he is small, a little frail, or really clumsy. Determine if the dog could use some help. Our older dog uses a set of portable plastic steps that we take everywhere, and I assist him in climbing the steps into the sidecar (he is both frail AND clumsy).

You can use the same command that you use to allow your dog into the car or up on the bed, perhaps "Ok get in" or "Fido, up." Give lots of praise and rewards for getting in. Then decide what your command will be for exiting the sidecar. *This is essential.* You never want your dog to exit the sidecar without your permission, and without you already standing next to the sidecar. Never let him get out while you are still on the bike, even if it is stopped and off. You must establish the expectation that, once in the sidecar, he is there until you tell him otherwise. Stopping for traffic lights, gas, and fast food should be easy if he knows this. Of course, you'll also have a harness to tie him into the sidecar, but a dog can still get into a tangled mess with the tie-ups if he doesn't understand the rules.

So, with the bike off, the sequence might go like this:

- Have dog sit and stay beside sidecar.
- Say "Fido, up!" and motion to show how to get in.
- Say "Good dog. Stay." Give a treat.
- Walk over to the bike and get on. Praise and treat.
- Wait a minute, then walk around to the sidecar. Treat again. Say "Ok, off," or "Ok, here" and motion him out of the sidecar. Lots of praise and treats. Repeat several more times.

Your dog should feel positive about the sidecar before the bike is ever started with him in it.

Now slowly up the ante with movement, with the **bike off**, like this:

- Have the dog sit and stay beside sidecar
- Say "Fido, up!" and motion to show him how to get in.
- Say "Good dog. Stay." Give a treat.

- While you are standing next to the sidecar, push the bike around slowly. Depending on the size of the rig you might need a helper.
- Give frequent praise and treats if your dog remains calm while the bike is being pushed. If your dog sits and stays in the sidecar, feeling the movement and not freaking out, great! Praise and treat. But if your dog is not paying attention, getting way too excited and climbing all over the sidecar, then take a time out. Go back to the basics and practice getting his attention with basic exercises such as "watch me" where you give praise and treats every time his eyes meet yours. Or try a down-stay in the sidecar to get him calm. You'll know when your dog is calm enough to move on to the next step.
- Wait a minute after stopping. Treat again. Say "Ok, off," or "Ok, here" and motion him out of the sidecar. Lots of praise and treats. Repeat several more times.

This is a good place to note that you might want to start out with a little bike and sidecar before you make a big investment, just in case your dog hates to ride, and also to practice sidecar riding yourself before your precious cargo is in the passenger seat. We used a Honda Trail 90 and a homemade sidecar, but if you have a tractor or ATV which your dog already rides, you can bet the dog will take to the sidecar just fine.

If you have the time and materials a mini-bike with a wood sidecar can make a wonderful training platform.

Next it's time to make things a little more challenging by starting up the bike. Make sure your dog has heard the bike start before and can remain calm when it starts. Practice starting the bike while your dog is standing nearby with a second handler or with the dog tied near you. Praise and treat when your dog is calm (**never** when your dog is excited). You are preparing for the time when your dog sits in the sidecar and you start 'er up. The sound should not come as a surprise. You don't want a startled dog at this point.

The sequence might go like this:

- Have Fido sit and stay beside the sidecar.
- Say "Fido, up!" and motion to show how to get in.
- Say "Good dog. Stay." Give a treat. Remember to act relaxed and happy, not somber and grouchy.
- Walk over to the bike and get on. Praise and treat.
- Have a trusted helper stand next to the sidecar to prevent crazy attempts at exits if the dog freaks out.

- Start the motorcycle but **do not move it**. Lots of praise and treats. If the dog is calm, move on to the rest of the sequence below. But if the dog seems anxious or scared or overly excited, turn off the engine. Be quiet – do not scold. Wait until the dog calms down.

Wait a minute, then walk around to the sidecar. Say "Ok, off, or Ok, here" and motion him out of the sidecar. Lots of praise and treats. Repeat the whole sequence until he dog can remain calm with the engine on. Eventually your dog will become desensitized to being so close to the loud engine. If not, maybe those custom pipes are just a wee bit too loud? Perhaps Fido (and the neighbors) might appreciate a quieter set of pipes. Just sayin' …

Now it's time to put it all together and get rolling. But *only around the yard.*

The sequence goes like this:

- Put a harness on your dog before you head out to the bike. Make sure it's not the first time he has worn the harness. Practice putting it on and off indoors, again with treats and praise. Heel your dog to the sidecar. Tell him to sit and stay beside the sidecar while you make sure there are no empty pop cans or loose screwdrivers rolling around in the sidecar, or bees nests, small tasty mice, or anything else that might flap around and scare him.
- Say "Fido, up!" Tie in the harness to your secure anchor points, as discussed in the next chapter.
- Say "Good dog. Stay." Praise and treat.
- Walk over to the bike and get on. Praise and treat.
- Start the bike. Be calm, not exuberant. This is a mellow biker thing. Praise and treat if the dog is calm.
- Ride around slowly in first gear. Is everything okay? Try second. If all is well, ride around for a few more minutes.
- Stop the bike, Turn it off. Remind your dog to stay. Walk around to the sidecar and say "Ok, off, or Ok, here" and call him out of the sidecar. Lots of celebration now, along the lines of "Yeah! Whose my little super-snout sidecar dog? You are – yes YOU are!" Praise, treat and repeat the whole thing a few times.

Now you are ready for the road. But take it slow, no highways nor high speeds at first. Work up to it once you have a pretty good idea that your dog is good to go.

## Precautions

Do you think your dog loves everybody? Is he like Will Rogers, who said "a stranger is just a friend I haven't met yet?" Let's hope so, because everybody will be wanting to touch your dog. As your dog comes to see the sidecar as his, along with all the treats and praise and attention from you, he may decide to become possessive of his sidecar. Keep an eye out for any behavior that might indicate that this is happening. If you have any inkling of discomfort, it is your responsibility to tell people, sternly if necessary, not to approach the dog. Remember, your job is to keep the dog safe at all times. Some people may take offense that they can't touch your dog. Too bad. If someone gets bit, you could lose your house and your dog could lose his life. Take this seriously, but it doesn't have to spoil your ride. Park away from crowds if Fido dislikes strangers.

Sidecars can be hot in the sun. Try to park in the shade so the floor doesn't get too hot. Consider covering the floorboards with a towel if you must park in the sun. Always carry water and a dish for your friend, and we advise bringing along one of those portable beach umbrellas that attach to the arm of a beach chair. This is great when you and Fido are stuck in the sun eating your Big Macs, with the nearest shade tree in the next state.

Remember to leave room for Fido to jump out or use his steps. It's embarrassing to park too close to other bikes then have to push the bike back out because you forgot the dog needs space to get out.

Your dog and you will face many distractions while riding. People will honk, wave, yell, and literally chase you down to get pictures and tell you how awesome you are. They will squeal and call your dog, and make whistling sounds, and in general scare the pants off you. It is most important to focus on keeping the motorcycle under control and safe, then focus on the dog, and only if you have any spare attention should you address the paparazzi.. Your dog should be tied in securely so that you needn't be distracted by concerns about him jumping out.

Hercules d'Boxer is ready for cool weather.
(JD "PupDaddy" Whitaker handler, used with permission)

Make sure your dog stays warm in winter. We recommend a fleece coat that zips under his belly to protect as much of his stomach as possible, since that's what faces the wind when he sits up. On top of the fleece you may put a lighter wind-resistant material like leather or nylon. And don't forget the Doggles!

**Doggles**

Ava "The Wing Mut" from South West Scotland shows off her Doggles. (photo Mike Easton, used with permission)

Doggles™ are a commercial brand of sunglasses designed to fit the shape of a dog's head. Doggles were invented by Roni Di Lullo for her dog MidKnight. Doggles are used by military dogs to protect them from desert sand, to protect some dogs that have eye conditions and by dogs that ride motorcycles for the same reason that humans wear eye protection on motorcycles.

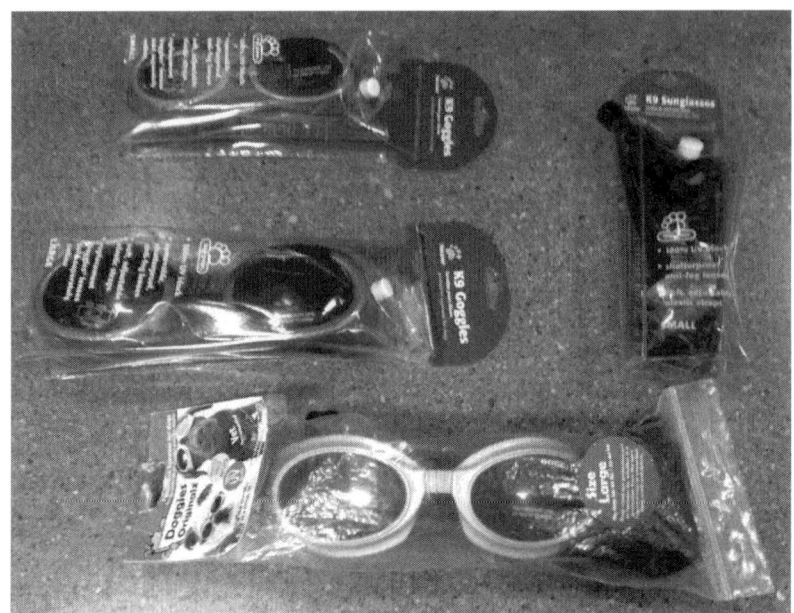

Doggles and dog sunglasses can protect your dog's eyes and reduce eye watering while riding.

These are a show stopper but are they really necessary? If you don't have a windshield on the sidecar, then yes, your dog needs Doggles. They will protect his eyes from wind, insects, and debris – the same reasons we wear them. Of course your dog probably doesn't know that and will not be amused at first.

If you simply make it clear from the start that Doggles are required for getting the bike to move, he'll catch on. Be consistent – don't take them off if he fusses and paws at them.

**Skills and Commands for Riding**

There are a few essential commands or skills that every sidecar dog should know well. These include "sit," "lie down," "stay," "up" or "get in," "off" or "out," "leave it" or "watch me," and leaving the Doggles on.

**Teaching the "Stay" Command**
In a place free of distractions, with your dog sitting and on leash, position your hand flat in front of his snout while saying "stay." Count to 10 then say "ok" and gesture for him to move toward you to receive a treat. If the dog moves before you release him, put him right back in position

wordlessly, but repeating your hand gesture. Don't repeat your verbal commands. Practice a few times every day, gradually increasing the time you keep him on a stay until he can successfully stay for 1 full minute. Then repeat, but this time have him lie down to stay.

After he is reliably staying for a minute, add some distractions to tempt him to disobey. Have someone sneakily roll a ball past his feet. Let the cat into the room. Have your child walk around making squeaky sounds. Quietly reward and treat (by walking over to the dog – don't let the dog walk toward the reward) as long as he holds the stay. But if he moves out of position, very quickly use the leash to get him back into it.

As he improves, have him lie down and stay throughout dinner, or while you watch a movie. He doesn't have to remain motionless, but he has to stay in the place where you told him to lie down. You can step on his leash during this time so he doesn't get up when you are distracted. Always release him with praise and a treat. A bomb-proof "stay" is useful when dealing with distractions in a sidecar!

**Teaching "Watch Me' or "Leave it"**

This awesome command gets the dog's attention (eyes) back on you, regardless of what shenanigans are going on elsewhere. Sit on the floor with your dog in a quiet room. Let your dog see you put some treats on the floor, and say "leave it" or "watch me" as you quickly cover them up with your hand. Most dogs will nose your hand and try to bite, claw or lick at your hand to get to the treats. Be strong – don't let him succeed. Eventually he will get frustrated and look at you in either annoyance or confusion. Say "yes" when he looks in your eyes, and give him a <u>better</u> treat that you happen to have squirreled away in your pocket. He will get the hang of this soon – ignore the food under your hand and look at your eyes instead.

Now – tempt him by removing your hand. The treats are right there taunting him from the ground. Will he go for them? Hopefully so. Just before his tongue can reach them, cup your hand over the treats and say "leave it" or "watch me". Argh! Fido is foiled again! But as he eventually looks up at your eyes, praise and treat with the superior treats.

How does this work in the real world? A cat is crossing the road. Fido sees it from the sidecar and gets himself all worked up to jump out. You say "Fido, leave it" and he looks straight at you for an instant, giving you the chance to whip out a tasty sidecar treat and distract him long enough for the cat to make a clean getaway.

## Dealing with Doggles

In a quiet room, hold out the Doggles If he sniffs them or looks at them say "good boy!" and offer a treat. Put them on for just a second and take them back off very quickly. Say "good dog!" and offer a treat. Gradually increase the amount of time you leave them on until he can wear them for up to a minute before you take them off. If he tries to take them off without you, say "no" and wait to the count of 10 before removing them. You don't want him to think he can get his way or hasten the process by helping take them off.

Put the Doggles on right before giving the bike throttle to take off, and take them off as soon as you turn off the engine. The dog should feel that the Doggles are part of riding, and he'll be too distracted to mess with them as long as you are moving. But they can be hot and itchy while sitting still, so don't make him wear them when the engine is off.

## Teaching Go Potty or Do Your Business Using Clicker Training

Some riders have found that teaching your dog to relieve himself on command is useful. Unlike kids, the dog can't tell you when he needs a potty break while on the open road, so he needs to go when you stop. Most dogs can muster up a little urine to mark a fence post or squat on a rival's pee spot anytime, so why not teach them to do it on command?

Clicker training is a fun way to teach this, and many other tricks and commands. We've really enjoyed this training method with our dogs, especially for tricks and other "fun" behaviors. There are many good books on the subject and we encourage you to try it out.

Once an owner learns clicker training, many new possibilities open up.
In general, the idea is that a well-timed "click" can tell a dog if he is "hot or cold" in figuring out what behavior you want from him. It's like saying "YES! – That's IT!" So get yourself a clicker at the pet store and try this:

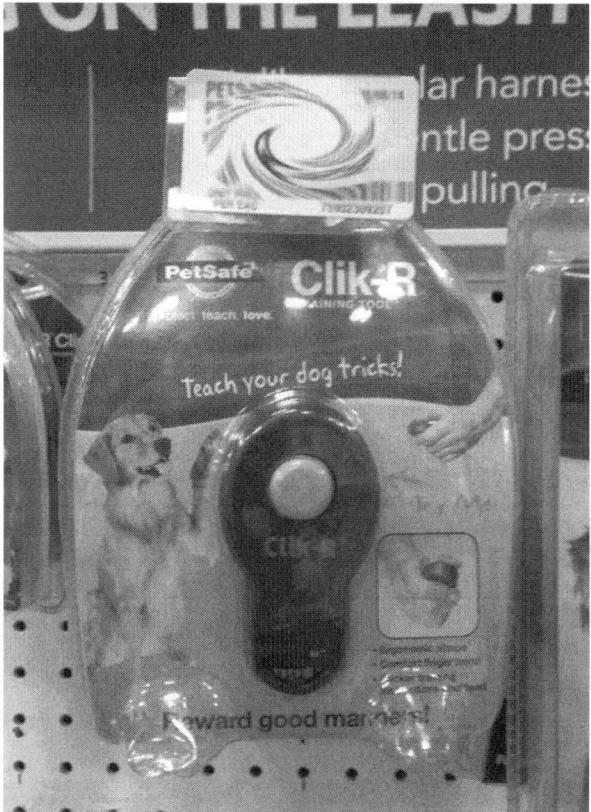

Clicker type training tools are fantastic aids.

Next time your dog lifts his leg or squats to pee outside, click the clicker and toss him a treat. He will look happy and confused. He'll come nosing you for more. Sorry, no more.

If he resumes peeing, click and treat again. But he might just be too distracted, or maybe he is all out of urine. That's fine. Continue with your day.

Next time you let him out or walk him, and he starts to pee, click and treat.

No need for words at this point.

Pretty soon he will either make sure he pees while you are watching, or he'll fake the pee stance by lifting his leg or squatting without peeing. As long as he is really peeing, click and treat. If he is fake-peeing you might ignore him. Start adding the phrase "go potty" or "do your business" right before you think he's going to pee. When he pees, click and treat. Pretty soon he'll be doing this reliably.

## Dog Training Dogma

There are as many opinions on dog training as there are on child rearing, and in both cases you'll find people judging your techniques. Every dog is unique and different techniques might be more appropriate in different circumstances. For instance, one of our dogs is so timid that any form of correction makes him lose focus and motivation. He isn't very bright so even the most basic clicker training frustrates him (and us). However, rewarding good behavior, ignoring bad, and luring him into positions such as down and sit work perfectly to train him.

Our other very brilliant dog loves clicker training, and we've taught him some truly impressive tricks this way. Likewise, luring with praise and treats was enough to get him excited about and well trained in the agility ring and in the sidecar. But he is a highly reactive and stubborn dog, and we need guaranteed obedience when it matters most. For this unconditional obedience we rely on traditional methods using attention corrections, and applying higher degrees of discomfort with an e-collar until he can't ignore us.

Cesar Millan is an example of a traditional trainer. Eventually, by using appropriate levels of punishment when he was not paying attention to us, we taught our dog that ignoring us is not worth it, no matter what trigger is provoking or exciting him. Did it work? It was the only thing that did. Did it "ruin his spirit" like some modern trainers would have you believe? Absolutely not! It made him more calm and relaxed to know that mom and dad were the toughest leaders around and that we would always keep him safe – all he needed to do was look at us and we'd be there dealing with the problem for him.

This kind of trust is essential when dealing with all the unknowns during a sidecar ride. When using traditional training, however, find an experienced trainer that you understand and trust. Ours was John Smith at All About Dogs in Cincinnati.

Our advice is to avoid dog training "dogma" and adopt a zen-like open-mindedness and flexibility to your training. You don't have to use just one method. Go to many trainers and classes, read lots of books on dog training techniques, and see what works best with your dog. Here are a few great books to get you started:

*The Thinking Dog – Crossover to Clicker Training* by Gail Tamases Fisher, Dogwise Publishing, Washington, U.S.A. 2009

*Don't Shoot the Dog* by Karen Pryor, Bantam Books 1999

*How to be the Leader of the Pack and Have Your Dog Love You for it!* by Patricia MCConnell, PhD. MCConnell Publishing, Ltd. Black Earth, WI. 1996

*The Other End of the Leash: Why We Do What We Do Around Dogs.* By Patricia McConnell, Ballantine Books, NY 2002

*How to Be Your Dog's Best Friend: The Classic Training Manual For Dog Owners* by the Monks of New Skete, 2002

A well trained dog makes for both a happy well-adjusted dog and happy owners.

# 3 SIDECAR OUTFITTING FOR DOGS (AND PERHAPS HUMANS)

**What a Dog NEEDs in a Sidecar**

No dog owner wants to cause pain or harm to their best friend.

It is the responsibly of the dog owner to thoroughly vet any sidecar for any issues that have a reasonable chance of doing harm to the dog.

Some issues are obvious while others take some time and consideration to discover and address.

Check for bolts, nuts, sharp corners and pad the sidecar.

It is critically important that you run your hands over and press on every surface inside the sidecar that your dog can reach. Even if you don't think it is likely that your dog will stand next to a certain surface, remember that driving is a dynamic process and your dog may get pushed into unexpected positions.

Bolt ends and seating mounts are common places of concern as they can be hard or even sharp surfaces that under the right circumstances can injure your dog while riding. Remediation of these issues is on a case by case basis; typically silicone glue and rubber matting can do an effective job.

A mat of some kind should be installed in the sidecar that provides a surface on which to stand, sit and lie that is both grippable and non-slippery but with at least some minor cushioning. Several fake leather mats approximately ½ inch thick are available that provide an ideal floor for most sidecars. These mats MUST be securely installed so they do not catch the wind and scare the dog or blow out of the sidecar. This can be done with "super magnets" (rare earth magnets), or non-hardening adhesives.

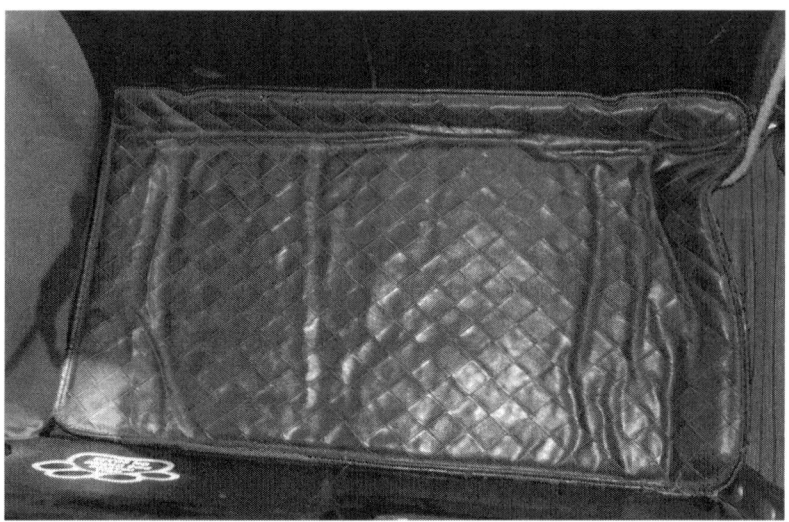

Mat choice is critical. It must not flap or rise up in the wind, it must provide padding and also a firm grip for the dog.

Our recommendation for sidecar floor mats are the chef's mats available at BigLots!™. They are anti-fatigue floormats that seem to add the right amount of cushion and traction for sidecar dog use. The price is about $15 and they can also be found on Amazon.com as a "Chef's Comfort Mat".

**Standing and Sitting**

Many people don't realize that it can be painful or even harmful for a dog to sit for long periods of time.

It is critically important for your sidecar and harness design to allow your dog to be able to sit, stand and lie down.

**Harness Design**

Arguably one of the more important and challenging things that must be used in the sidecar for your dog is a safety harness.

Why a safety harness? Some people don't use safety harnesses because they want the dog to be able to be thrown free in the case of an accident. That is not what we recommend because too many times we have seen our dogs caught by surprise when a quick stop or sharp turn happens while the dog is distracted. If these events had happened with no harness installed the dogs could have been injured or killed.

An ideal harness design would include an adjustable break-away system that could contain the dog during normal turns and lunges but would release the dog in the event of an accident. As of the date of this writing we have found no commercial product that does this. Should we find a product that does we will post it on this book's webpage or social media page(s). If you know about such a product please let us know. One product we found by "SleepyPod" appeared to be such a product but after examination turned out to be no more effective than a rigid harness system. A number of owners that ride with dogs have attempted to design breakaway systems but to our knowledge none have been tested in a "crash test dummy" system to verify effectiveness.

An additional helpful harness feature is a grip or handle on the back of the harness to help you to grab the harness if you need to help reposition the dog.

One of the most critical mistakes to avoid is attaching a secured leash line to the dog's collar. NEVER attach a secured or tied down line to the dog's collar. Even small unexpected jolts can cause serious injury to your dog's neck and spine. Always connect secured lines and tied down leashes to a 4-point chest or back harness.

The best harness design is a 3 or 4-point harness with a connection ring in the front chest area of the dog. Having the secured line or leash connection on a front harness ring provides the most flexibility of moment for the dog, offers the least chance of neck or back injury and allows for a number of connection mounting points on the sidecar.

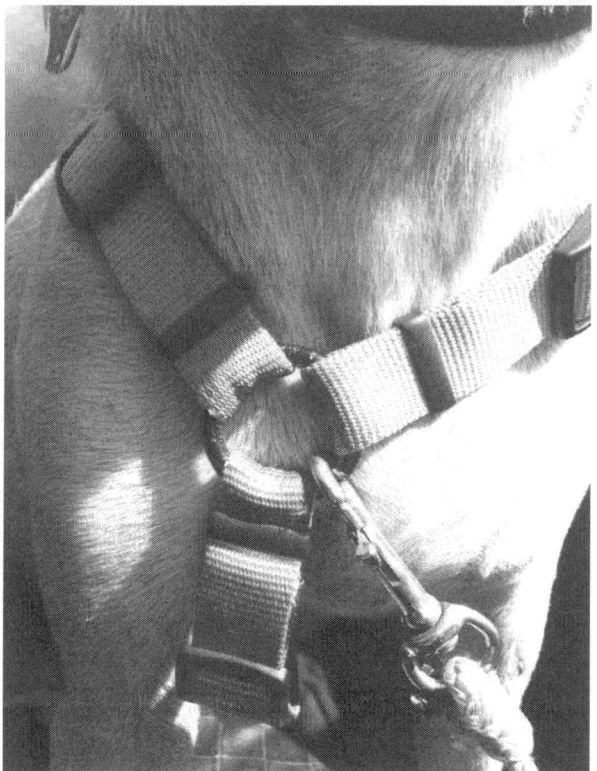

A 3 or 4 point harness with a front ring provides some of the best options for safety. NEVER attach a line to the dogs collar.

One of the best commercial harnesses on the market for sidecar use is the KONG® Comfort Dog Harness & Traffic Loop. Available in a large range of sizes and colors this sturdy harness has ideal front and back ring attachments. Additionally, the KONG harness has a sturdy handle on the back, that is helpful if you need to reach over and gain control of the dog, and is readily available at most large pet retailers and online.

The second part of the harness is the system that attaches it to the sidecar. As previously stated this system must be configured in such a way to allow the dog to sit, stand or lie-down.

In the most basic system, a ring bolt (eyebolt) is installed in the bottom of the sidecar in front of the dog on the motorcycle side of the car. A short leash or rope with clip is attached to the ring after careful testing with the dog to confirm the dog's range of movement.

Harness system eyebolts should be securely attached with no sharp edges.

If the dog tends to get tangled up or turned around, a second mount point and rope can be added at another location to restrict the dog's sideways movement. The second rope or leash can be attached to the front harness ring or if your harness has an additional ring on the back of the harness that may prove useful as well.

Once the harness system you design is well tested it is important to make sure you get into the habit of securing the dog right away each time the dog enters the sidecar so that you don't get distracted and forget.

**Entering and Exiting the Sidecar**

Just as a safe and comfortable environment must be provided for the dog inside of the sidecar, you must also make sure the dog can get in and out without injury or undue stress. If the dog is uncomfortable or afraid he will grow to dislike the sidecar.

An ideal sidecar will allow the dog to easily enter and exit with little to no modifications. Many sidecars have a low point, known as a step through, which the dog can use to access the interior of the sidecar and often sidecars have a step mounted in front of the fender to assist entry.

Unfortunately, many sidecars do not have a step or step through and to enter or exit your dog will have to jump several feet. This kind of system is usable for a young and agile dog but does present a number of drawbacks. No matter how agile your dog is, he could possibly make a mistake and misjudge his jump, causing him to be injured or frightened and possibly turning him off to sidecar riding. As your dog ages it will eventually become more difficult and painful for your dog to perform these large jumps and hopefully he and you do not discover this the hard way.

Some sidecars are difficult for dogs to enter and exit. Adding carpet or a graspable surface to the sloped back of this sidecar might make it dog friendly.

If you are unwilling or unable to modify the existing sidecar to allow walk-in access for the dog, a possible alternative is a step system. A set of sturdy but light foldable stairs can be used to give your dog access in and out of the sidecar and then strapped or secured to the sidecar for transport. One example we have used with success is the Solvit PupStep Plus. Another alternative is to simply lift your dog in and out of the sidecar assuming your dog is light enough and your back strong enough.

A set of Solvit PupStep steps help an aging dog in and out of a Velorex sidecar

## What Your Dog WANTS in a Sidecar

Dogs can appreciate accessories and conveniences just like we can. Having a storage area or an accessories bag in the sidecar or motorcycle stocked with water, collapsible water dish, extra leashes, doggie do-do bags, towels, and storage and lens cleaner for the Doggles is a great idea.

If there is no storage already built into your sidecar, automotive organizers and storage bags could come in handy. Auto and truck organizers designed to fit between the seats of a car or truck often fit nicely in the front or back of a sidecar and provide storage for dog accessories and perhaps even some human accessories. One example would be the Adeco Seat and Trunk Car Vehicle Organizer, available online for about $25. One critical aspect of using an organizer is that it must be secured from shifting around in the sidecar and any contents it holds must be stowed in such a way they are unlikely to get caught by the wind and depart the organizer.

Automotive organizers can provide great storage for Doggles, water dishes, water, leashes and other items needed in dog friendly travels.

Even on short trips you should be proactive about bringing water or other essentials in case of a mechanical breakdown.

On hot summer days a breakdown could leave you and your dog in direct sun over hot asphalt. Even if you don't break down, while you are out of the sidecar shopping, attending an event or walking your dog your sidecar could become baking hot in the sun. Keeping a towel in storage and laying the towel down on the sidecar floor will go a long way to protect your dog from getting into a solar powered frying pan for the ride home.

While we do not recommend leaving your dog in the sidecar unattended there are times when you may wish to leave the dog in the sidecar while you are nearby. If shaded parking is not available this could pose a problem on hot days. One solution is to use a clamp-on portable umbrella like those made for folding chairs. Clamp the umbrella onto the sidecar or motorcycle and adjust it to provide shade for the dog and the floor of the sidecar. Our favorite is the Rio Beach Total Sun Block My Shade Clamp-On Umbrella for about $15.

## Weights

Depending on the weight of your dog and the configuration of your rig, you may want or need to add weight to your sidecar. Sandbags used by photographers to secure lighting equipment are inexpensive and nearly ideal for this. If more than one sandbag is needed put them together into a pillow case making a soft single bag that can be secured with a grommet. If your sidecar has separate storage, place them in the storage area. If your sidecar does not have storage be sure the bags will not fly or shift during hard braking or an accident.

Photographer's equipment sandbags make versatile weight systems. Filling them with pea gravel works well and keeps sand out of your rig.

## Weather Protection

While the majority of riders are only fair weather friends to their motorcycles some people ride in nearly all conditions. Adventure riders or touring riders that plan on taking their dog along on a sidecar have the added responsibly of making sure the dog is as well-equipped and comfortable as they are.

There is a craze of dog accessories in the US and UK right now and items such as heated vests, dog coats and even pet camping supplies are readily available.

When riding in the cold and wind with a short haired dog, or any dog that does not like the cold, consider a vest or coat. Avoid the "fashion" coats sold for dog dress up events and seek out vests and coats made of the same materials you would use yourself.

If you do cold weather or winter riding, you know that it does not matter what your coat or jacket is made of if the wind gets in. Apply this same knowledge to outfitting your dog for weather. A fashionable hood on the back of a coat that gets caught in the wind and flutters or an open collar that lets air billow in will not serve your dog well.

Our tried and true recommendation for a short haired dog is the Ruffwear Climate Changer Dog Coat for about $80. This Ruffwear dog coat zips securely and provides full coverage for the dogs underside.

For winter riding with a short haired dog, the key features to look for in a coat are chest coverage and sealing out wind.

## Pre-ride Checklist

Over time tires wear, mounts stress, harnesses and ropes wear. The responsible rider will always check the condition of the rig on a regular basis, ideally before each trip. Make sure that the sidecar mount is not missing any cotter pins, has not slipped in adjustment, has no cracks. Check tires for tread and inflation. Remember that tires on sidecar rigs wear FAST.

Tires can wear quickly on sidecar rigs.

**Treats in the Sidecar**

If your dog knows there is food in the sidecar, he may become possessive of the sidecar and act aggressively toward others that approach the sidecar.

It's likely you will want to have treats available for sidecar training, to reinforce your dog's tolerance of wearing his Doggles, for distraction control or just because you like to treat your dog. You may want to consider keeping the treats on your person or in a pocket or place on your motorcycle away from where your dog may become possessive of it, but yet easy for you to reach.

It is a good idea have a place to store treats that are accessible at stop lights but make sure your dog does not become possessive of the bike.

## What Your Dog DOES NOT Want in a Sidecar

There should never be any reason for your dog to become spooked, uncomfortable or injured by loose objects in the sidecar.

Large and small loose objects can frighten a dog that is strapped in to a sidecar and wearing Doggles. Keep all objects secured.

When your dog is strapped into the sidecar with Doggles on, his vision and movement are limited. Something as simple as a crumpled paper towel whipping around in the air inside the sidecar could spook your dog into injuring himself or at the very least becoming uncomfortable and disliking sidecar riding.

A rattling object in the sidecar such as loose bolt, flapping bungee cord or rattling cans or tools can cause discomfort for your dog. Be courteous and think about the ride from your dog's point of view and reevaluate this for each ride.

**Windshields**

If your sidecar has a vintage GLASS windshield remove it. Vintage glass windshields are unsafe for any occupant -- human or dog.

Modern Lexan or Plexiglas windshields will not shatter into sharp glass pieces and they offer protection from the wind. However, does your dog want protection from the wind?

If you observe dogs riding in sidecars, or cars and trucks for that matter, almost universally they want to get their face into the wind and don't want to sit behind the windshield the majority of the time.

Some riders leave the windshield in place and let the dog put his head on either side of the windshield during riding. In many cases this may be uncomfortable for the dog. Think about how long you could look 90 degrees out of a truck or train window before your neck and back got sore?

If you are able to, remove the windshield or take it to a place that does Plexiglas or Lexan finishing and have it reshaped or shortened.

If you need to keep the windshield in place because it is required for a cover or top then try to make sure your dog has room to look out of the side comfortably.

If the tall windshield is required for a vinyl roof you will not be able to remove or reshape it.

## Riding at Night with Your Dog

When we started riding home at night from events, we were both shocked and startled by what appeared to be dogs disappearing from the sidecars!

At night the dark inside of a sidecar can hide even a light tan dog completely, especially when there are some external lights shining from the road.

To explain this effect, think of looking at the front of a car at night when its headlights are on. Can you tell the color of the car or even its shape? No, the headlights remove all contrast from anything outside of the light cone.

It is the riders responsibility to be able to monitor the dogs situation in the sidecar and if you cannot see the dog, this ability is compromised or removed.

There are several ways to remedy this situation.

One is to install permanent lighting into the interior of the sidecar. Permanent lighting does not rely on a battery and can be designed to be controlled from the riders position while driving.

An easier, less expensive option is to buy battery powered LED lights that can be affixed to the inside of the sidecar and turned on and off before and after night operations.

Another fun and helpful option are LED lighted dog collars. LED lighted collars make the dog more visible and even makes your rig more visible to other drivers. Can find these at pet stores around Halloween or online year round.

LED lighted collars are a fun easy way to see your dog in the sidecar at night.

# 4 CHOOSING A RIG

A "rig," also called an "outfit" is a motorcycle and sidecar combination. So in other words once you have a sidecar attached to a motorcycle the complete vehicle is now called a sidecar rig or just rig.

This chapter is about purchasing a rig that is already assembled. If you plan to purchase the motorcycle (mule) and sidecar (hack) separately and attach them, see chapters 5 and 6.

Complete rigs fall into three categories: factory rig, dealer rig, custom rig.

**Factory Rigs**

A factory rig was designed by the MOTORCYCLE manufacturer and sold through a motorcycle dealer.

The most common examples are (USA) Harley Davidson, (International) Ural, CJ750.

Factory rigs have a number of advantages because the mounting system was designed by the motorcycle manufacturer when the motorcycle was created, not as an aftermarket afterthought.

**Factory Rigs – Harley Davidson**

Harley Davidson produced factory sidecar rigs from 1927 through 2011. They have stopped selling and producing the Harley factory rigs but they still service and support the product. With a little luck and research you can likely still get a factory Harley rig used from a dealership.

Harley factory sidecar rigs are large "Dreadnaught Class" machines and are made with some of the largest motorcycles Harley Davidson produced. These sidecars are sturdy and have plenty of power, speed and durability for long cross country tips. If you are looking for a factory made rig that is fully capable of interstate highway touring this is it.

Harley Davidson sidecar rigs are well designed, include sidecar wheel brakes and hold a good reputation. The Harley sidecars are light but with strong sub-frames employing specially designed connections for the Harley Davidson motorcycles.

There are not many downsides to modern Harley Davidson rigs except perhaps the price. Modern Harley rigs keep a steep resale value which is good when you own one but not so good when you are buying one.

Vintage factory Harley Davidson sidecar rigs, however, come with the reliably and maintenance issues associated with that particular generation of motorcycle. Some older generations of Harley Davidson motorcycles are famous for mechanical issues and these should be avoided unless you have done your homework.

Terry White with his pack Willie G, Lizzy and Harley riding a Harley Davidson motorcycle with Harley Davidson sidecar.

**Factory Rigs – Ural**

Ural motorcycles have dealerships in the USA and around the world. Unlike Harley Davidson, most Urals are sold with a sidecar.

Ural motorcycles were designed from the ground up to carry a sidecar so dealers, manuals and other resources all support the rig format.

Older generations of Ural motorcycles, like a few of the older generations of Harley Davidson motorcycles, have a reputation of poor reliability. However the reasons for this are somewhat different.

Ural motorcycles are a design derived from pre-World War II BMW motorcycles. The motorcycle design, suspension and sub-frame bears only a mild resemblance to its BMW forefathers but the sidecar body is still nearly the same.

Tom Well's dog Archie riding a Ural on a journey around the northwest US. (photo used with permission)

Nearly every BMW model ever made has been highly reliable so what happened with the middle aged Urals?

The BMW models from which the Ural was derived were created before 65 mph interstate highways. The pre-war BMW motorcycles were made with 1930s technology for 1930s roads.

It took the Ural company a little while to transition their bikes and work out the kinks for the emissions standards required for US imports and to modify the bikes for modern US road systems as opposed to the dirt and gravel country roads for which they were originally designed.

Urals are now hands-down the most popular factory made sidecar rigs.

A brand-new Ural will likely cost only a portion of a used Harley Davidson or Honda Goldwing professionally designed rig.

With Urals favorably priced, factory dealer supported, and very popular it is hard not to recommend them as a great rig for you and your dog.

The Ural sidecar is easy for all dogs, even older ones to get in and out of, offers lots of room, great storage, a rack or spare tire mount and can be easily modified to support both dog and human passengers. Furthermore, Urals are available in a number of styles from a classic vintage configuration to a modern adventure ATV with a powered sidecar wheel (the motorcycle world equivalent of a 4x4 off road vehicle).

Urals, Zundapps and some other makes have the option of a powered sidecar wheel making them a fantastic off-road vehicle.

Wait, the Ural features still don't stop there. Ural motorcycles have a leading-link fork (known to BMW fans as an Earles Fork) that is specifically designed to take the effort out of controlling a heavy rig and the sidecar is outfitted with a modern adjustable suspension system.

Should you drop this book and go buy a Ural today? Perhaps, but there are a few limitations to the Ural sidecar rig nirvana.

The first important limitation to know about Ural configurations is that the factory specified top sustained (cruising) speed is only 70 mph and I assume that is an empty or lightly loaded rig on straight and level roads.

In a realistic highway environment you can expect your 2008 or newer Ural to run in the range of about 55 mph up hills and 70 on the straight and level. Urals produced before 2008 may run about 5-10 mph under this.

For some people this kind of performance is great, especially if your interstate highway travels are limited. If you want the ability to keep up with traffic on 65 and 75 mph interstates then perhaps a Ural is not for you.

Don't let this give you the impression that if you get a Ural you cannot participate in long cross country traveling. Many Ural owners travel long distances akin to those for which BMW owners are famous.

The second thing to consider is that even though they have received many modern upgrades and are very sturdy machines, especially the 2008 and newer models, they still have one foot in the 1940's. This means you can expect to do more frequent tune ups and trips to the dealer for maintenance than, say, a new Honda.

If your riding will be primarily on trips that do not include 65 mph or faster interstate highways and you would like a sturdy outfit it is hard to beat the "bang for the buck" you get from a late model Ural. The Ural's option to have a powered wheel on the sidecar makes it a top choice for off-road or wintery conditions.

## Factory Rigs – CJ750

As previously mentioned the Ural rigs have a history rooted in pre-World War II motorcycles. The Chinese Chang Jiang 750, unlike the modern Ural, is for most practical purposes little changed from a 1930s flat-head, side-valve, 24 horsepower BMW.

CJ750's are sometimes called a BMW "copy" but this is not true. Technically the CJ750 is a BMW R71 derivative licensed BMW, some of which were even produced from the original German tooling. The BMW R71 motorcycle has the longest production life of any motorcycle starting in Germany in the 1930s, moving by war reparations act treaty to Russia as the M72, then to China as the CJ750. Although a great deal of the history of the origins of these bikes was lost during the war, Peter J Ballard's exhaustive research provides strong evidence that early M72/CJ750s are a true licensed BMW motorcycle.

When Germany gave up the BMW R71 license and production as part of war reparations, the technology spread around the planet, as this was one of the most advanced motorcycles of the day. Nearly every major motorcycle manufacturer took on some of the technology such as sprung frames, foot shifting, hand clutch and other advanced features. Harley Davidson even made a clone called the XA.

This planted the seeds for dozens of motorcycles with integrated sidecars, some still produced today such as the Ural.

PLA (Peoples Liberation Army) CJ750s, unlike the heavily evolved Urals, can be difficult to distinguish from 1930s German-made BMW R71s. For this reason they are a favorite for war re-enactors as an $8000 CJ750 is less of an investment to drive through fields and mud then a $60,000 R12 or R71.

Rob Crowder and his dog Brody riding a late model overhead valve CJ750. (used with permission)

As time moved into the 1980s even the Chinese started to improve the original R71 design, adding overhead valves and 12-volt electrical systems.

So is a CJ750 motorcycle for you?

We cannot recommend CJ750s as a sidecar rig for everyone.

CJ750 rigs require frequent care and maintenance that, to be affordable, typically must be done by the owner. Because 1930s motorcycles were not designed to be driven on modern asphalt roads they will have to be modified to stop seal ruptures and other problems. The realistic top sustained cruising speed is about 45 mph and the drum braking system is arguably dangerous on modern roads.

If you want to ride a CJ750 you will need to become familiar with maintaining a 1930s era motorcycle.

If you like vintage motorcycles, plan on driving mostly locally, want something very unique to drive, like to do your own maintenance and you have a fair amount of patience there are some positive aspects to owning a CJ750.

If you want something very unique to drive with your dog then this is a great rig. The technology used is dead simple and straight forward so if you want to learn to rebuild BMW boxer engines CJ750's might be a cheap good place to start. The Chinese made tons of parts (yes tons) that are still wrapped in wax in warehouses in China. Although shipping takes a while, the parts are inexpensive and readily available from several vendors fluent in English. Manuals and help with service can be had on the internet. You can do 98% of the service using the original 1938 BMW manuals as the bikes have changed so little.

If you dare to wade into the waters of CJ750 ownership we do have some advice for you. If you do manage to rebuild a vintage CJ750 for your regular rig you may find that despite the shortcomings it can be a wonderful workhorse motorcycle to own. Our CJ750 is part of the family, and affectionately called "The China Girl." Out of the many dozens of motorcycles we have owned the China Girl easily ranks in the top five of our all-time favorites.

Our advice for CJ750 ownership is the following: For the most vintage look, go with the SV (Side Valve) flat head bikes. Older is better as the original PLA parts and bikes tended to have better quality control. The brakes are terrible and hard to make better without losing the vintage look. You will need to learn to adjust your driving habits so that you have plenty of room to stop in all circumstances. When you get your bike, do a ground up rebuild and always do a "pre-flight" check of the rig before and after each ride. Deep oil sumps, modified final drive breathers, Valvoline 50wt Racing Oil and heat reducing carburetor intake manifolds are a must on modern roads.

## Factory Rigs – Royal Enfield

Royal Enfields have an amazing history. These bikes were produced in England and spawned an Indian "subsidiary." When the plant in England closed in the early 1970s the Indian factory continued to produce motorcycles under the original UK license, much like what we saw in the BMW/CJ750 history.

Indian-made Royal Enfields are now available from dealers in the USA and offer a unique way to buy a vintage motorcycle that is brand new. The Royal Enfields required some "upgrading" to meet US Department of Transportation standards, however they are still a great classic motorbike. If you live in California your Royal Enfield options could be limited by California's more stringent emissions standards so if you live in this state you might have some homework to do.

The Royal Enfield offerings at the time of this writing are principally the 535cc, 4-stroke, single cylinder line. While Royal Enfield does not produce their own sidecars the dealerships are partnering with sidecar manufacturers to reproduce the vintage factory rigs of the past. In the USA Cozy sidecars can be installed by dealers and Watsonian in the UK.

Like the Ural rigs, Royal Enfield motorcycles won't fare well at US interstate highway speeds. As a rule of thumb 500cc motorcycles with a sidecar should top out at about 65mph max. Urals have a bit more displacement but also more weight.

If you are not looking for a vintage-like single cylinder powered motorcycle rig, the Royal Enfield does not have much more going for it in terms of recommendations. Although you can get the rigs through the motorcycle dealer, it is no longer a true "factory" rig. In reality you are really working with a sidecar vendor that has an agreement with Royal Enfield.

**Hybrids and Conversions**

Most motorcycle manufacturers that once made motorcycles designed to carry a sidecar switched to making lightweight bikes that were not designed to carry sidecars in the late 1960s. One notable manufacturer continued producing full sidecar rigs, Ural. Until recently, Urals were considered high maintenance machines and could not keep up in modern traffic.

One method for solving this dilemma is the hybrid or conversion rig. Several dealers specialize in taking older frames from the 1950s and 1960s or Ural frames and replacing the engine with a much younger motorcycle engine. The result, if successful, is a tried and true frame made to carry a sidecar with a reliable up to date power plant that can handle modern roads.

Going for the best of both worlds. A CJ750 frame with a modern BMW airhead engine installed.

This best of both worlds approach has some sound reasoning but as with any customized motorcycle doing your research and finding a dealer with a good reputation is critical.

**Dealer Rigs**

Sidecar dealers and manufacturers will often buy factory new or used motorcycles and then sell them as a completed unit.

There are lots of advantages to this arrangement because the sidecar experts pair the motorcycle and sidecar together. Sidecar design and setup is a complicated and subtle science that does not favor the beginner or non-engineer.

The next advantage is that (hopefully) the complete rig you purchase from a sidecar dealer is very much like a number of other nearly identical rigs that have had any major bugs and problems discovered and resolved.

Sidecar dealer/manufacturer prepared rigs often have the motorcycle very well matched to the sidecar, not only in weight and balance but also in look, color, fit and finish.

As with any industry it is up to the buyer to research the reputation of the dealer in advance for its ratings on safety, customer service, reliability and cost.

Just as we recommend when buying any rig, it is important to have a general knowledge of what you want and what pros and cons each design choice brings. We would recommend you read the next two chapters on choosing motorcycles (mule) and sidecars (hack) before meeting with and evaluating the products of sidecar dealers or manufacturers that sell complete rigs.

# 5 CHOOSING THE MULE

The motorcycle that is chosen to pull a sidecar is often referred to as a "Tow Mule" or just "mule". Because motorcycles and sidecars have come in and out of fashion across many countries and languages since the early 1900s there are a great many variations of industry terms and slang. Outfits and rigs typically are terms that refer to a complete motorcycle and sidecar vehicle. Lots of terms are used to refer to the sidecars themselves; hacks, cars, carts, and bins. We decided to name this chapter after our favorite term for a sidecar-pulling motorcycle: "The Mule".

We strongly recommend not buying a motorcycle and sidecar then attaching the two and learning to ride by yourself.

The purpose of this chapter and the next is to discuss the features and general limitations of motorcycles and sidecars and to assist you in shopping for an already completed used or new rig.

There is an exception to every rule and with sidecar rigs that is also true, yet it is still a good idea to know the rules of thumb. So here we have compiled some of the general behaviors, features and good to know tidbits about choosing and buying a rig.

Most rigs will pull toward the sidecar on hard acceleration and pull away from the sidecar on hard braking. This is normal and it is an unusual setup if it does not exhibit at least some of this tendency at some weight/speed combination.

Vintage motorcycles are enjoyable if you don't mind doing the maintenance. (Warren Mann working on a 1952 Zundapp KS601)

Lots of motorcycle components will be under more strain when a sidecar is attached then they are designed for. In addition to the tires you can expect strain on the front forks, swing arm, and drive train.

Most rigs will eat tires for lunch. A sidecar outfit will almost always wear through tires much faster than a solo bike. Typically the back tire of the motorcycle, the sidecar tire, or both will experience a good deal of wear. Excessive tire wear is not necessarily a problem, as this is likely the price you pay for having a rig that behaves well in a large range of speeds and loads. However, if tire wear is just crazy, consult your sidecar shop or dealer.

The front forks of your motorcycle are a serious concern. Typically motorcycle front forks are not designed to turn the bike in the same manner as they are in a sidecar rig and also not designed for heavy side loading. Damage to your front forks can cause a reduction or loss of control.

The generally accepted best type of front fork for a mule is the leading link type. Vintage BMW fans know the leading link fork as the Earles Fork design. Most motorcycles sold today employ a telescopic fork design with the exception being the Ural.

If the mule has a telescopic fork it would be a good idea to consult your dealer/installer about installing a fork brace. Fork braces beef up the strength of the front forks to reduce damaging twisting forces.

Your front forks in many cases should also have a steering dampener installed. Sidecar loads can create harmonics that can cause "tank slap," a sometimes violent vibration in the forks from side to side. A steering dampener removes the ability of the forks to enter a dangerous degree of tank slap. Many stock solo motorcycles come with steering dampeners installed.

Additional strain will be placed on the motorcycle swing arm and drive train once a sidecar is added, but typically little can be done to beef up these components. Regular maintenance, ensuring you have good swing arm bearings and a reasonable driving style all help keep these parts of your bike functioning well.

Because of the extra load placed on the motorcycle engine any adjustments or additions that can aid the engine in torque and cooling should be examined, especially in the case of highway-going large displacement machines.

For shaft-driven motorcycles, find out if a sidecar final drive is available for your motorcycle. BMW and some other manufactures offered final drive gear ratios matched to the needs of a bike carrying a sidecar.

For chain driven motorcycles, obviously increased chain wear and capacity is an important concern but you may also wish to consider changing the number of teeth on the rear or front sprocket to give your bike more torque or "bite". If you find you are often over-revving or stalling your bike on take-off, especially on hills, or straining the engine on steep grades, chances are that manipulating your sprocket sizes can make for a better ride.

One of the most practical additions are oil cooling or capacity enhancements. Motorcycle manufacturers and aftermarket companies often sell deep oil pans (sump), oil temperature gauges and larger or add-on oil coolers.

A good example of a helpful aftermarket add-on is Randakk cycles's spin-on oil filter adapter and oil cooler kit. The kit replaces the stock Honda proprietary filter and allows you to use common automotive oil filters found at nearly every auto parts store. Additionally, because you can choose a much larger filter you add oil capacity and most importantly a port for installing an oil cooler. The addition of this kit to our Honda GL1000 with Velorex 700 sidecar brought the temperature of the engine coolant down from the top limit back into normal operating ranges when driving through the Kentucky foothills.

If your motorcycle already has an oil cooler but its mounting does not allow you to increase its size, consider splicing another oil cooler into the circuit and placing the second oil cooler in front of the original or perhaps in the airflow, such as between the bike and the sidecar.

When modifying oil coolers and lines it is imperative to use appropriate hose types, hose connections and if required, have a shop with the correct equipment crimp the hose end connectors. A scalding hot oil stream breaking open is not only dangerous to the health of the engine but also to the rider and passengers.

**Knowing What You Want**

Before you go hunting for a rig, it is important to have already worked out what kind of riding you plan on doing. If you plan on only local riding at or under 50 mph then you have a wide range of very good choices. However, if you want to travel on the interstate highway system and keep up with traffic, your options go down dramatically ( and likewise price goes up).

A 250cc 1960s Puch Motorcycle with a vintage Velorex (Jawa) sidecar looks like a work of art but islimited to non-interstate highway use. (designed and owned by Tom and Anne Kean)

A solo motorcycle at or above 500cc in size is typically able to keep up in highway traffic, be reasonably comfortable at speed and able to handle steep inclines.

For a motorcycle with a sidecar attached we would recommend 1000cc engines as the starting point for an interstate highway capable rig.

If this is your first sidecar rig, which we assume is the case for the majority of readers, you will want a well behaved rig that does not get "squirrely" during sharp turns. Tall motorcycle sidecar combinations require more work to balance because the center of gravity (CG) is located higher off of the ground, making the rig easier to tip. If a rig looks tall with lots of ground clearance be sure it has been assembled by a good shop and has been rechecked to be stable.

**Why so many BMWs?**

It won't take long when shopping for sidecar rigs to notice that BMW or BMW-related motorcycles (CJ, Ural, Dnepr, Zundapp, IMZ) make up a large percentage of the mules. Why is this?

German bikes such as the Zundapp KS750 brought many innovations to motorcycling especially for sidecars. The KS750 or "Germany's JEEP" was never produced as a solo bike; it was the first motorcycle with hydraulic brakes, two wheel drive and reverse.

BMW manufactured motorcycles were designed from the factory to carry sidecars, with factory installed and welded connection points, throughout their history all the way up until 1970. Even solo bikes generally had factory sidecar connection points on the frame and were prewired with an electrical connection port for a sidecar to plug right in.

After 1970 BMW stopped producing bikes with factory sidecar connection points and included notices in owner manuals stating that the motorcycles were not designed to pull a sidecar. However, many of the traits that make a good mule have continued on even into today's modern BMW motorcycles.

It is not uncommon for even late model BMW motorcycles to have factory steering dampeners, sturdy frames, drive trains, beefy swing arms or other traits that make for a good mule, especially the "R" line of BMW motorcycles.

Lastly, BMW motorcycle riders' culture tends to lean more toward an adventure-rider lifestyle, so for a certain percentage of these riders, sidecars are a natural extension of their riding lives.

Spirit is an adventure-rider dog. Along with owner Ara Gureghian, Spirit and their BMW have traveled to many remote places. You can read about their adventures in the book *Freedom on Both Ends of the Leash*. (photo used with permission)

**Is there any bike that is not a good mule?**

People will put a sidecar on anything if challenged. But that does not mean it is a good idea.

A good mule is one that the installer recommends and is comfortable installing. You don't want to buy a motorcycle and not be able to find an experienced installer that is willing to put a sidecar on it for you.

In our experience some installers recommend 1980s cruisers and "standard" style motorcycles for inexpensive general mules. Other installers are very picky and will only consider installing sidecars on motorcycles that are on a strict list of approved brands and models.

In general here are some of the things you want to be thinking about:

The sidecar is going to have to attach to the motorcycle in typically four or more places. Therefore, access to the frame of the bike in several places will be needed on the side on which the sidecar will be installed. In many cases with newer more modern bikes this means that some of the body panels will need to be modified or removed.

Plastic body panels may need to be modified for the bike to accept sidecar mounts.

Some new motorcycle designs don't even have traditional frames and employ the engine and transmission case as part of the frame.

If you do some research you might find that the sidecar you would like to buy can be purchased with a specialized mount for a particular brand or line of motorcycles such as Harley Davidson or BMW. This makes things much easier as then you know what range of bikes to hunt for when shopping for a mule.

Do NOT assume that a "universal sidecar mount" will work with any motorcycle. Also do not assume that you even necessarily want to use a universal mount,; we will cover that more in the next chapter.

Use the internet to your advantage and see if you can find not just one but a number of people that use the particular motorcycle you are researching for a mule. Keep in mind that owner pride sometimes causes people to give a more glowing review than would a dispassionate observer.

# 6 CHOOSING A HACK

Just as there are many terms throughout history for the motorcycle that pulls a sidecar, there are also numerous terms for the sidecar itself. Among the many terms for the sidecar, "hack" is one of the more common, so we chose that term for this chapter.

Because this is a book primarily about dogs riding sidecars, we are going to assume that the primary purpose of your sidecar will be to transport your dog. However, it can be useful to have a duel purpose hack that can support an occasional human occupant.

Since the majority of commercial hacks were made to carry humans it does not seem like this would be much of a problem, yet there may be more consideration required then you think.

Many sidecar designs originate from pre-1970s Europe. Today especially in the USA people tend to have larger frames and larger waistlines and may not be able to comfortably fit into many of these designs or may exceed the structural capacity of some of the lighter designs. Also, the sidecar seat is typically removed and replaced with a structure for a dog's safety and comfort. Making the human and dog equipment easily and quickly interchangeable can cause a number of design constraints.

With that in mind let's look at some of the most important questions you will need to answer before shopping for a hack.

- Will you be traveling on interstate highways? (65+ mph)
- What size motorcycle do you plan to attach the hack to?

- Will this be a dog-only hack?
- What is your budget?
- Do you want to be able to cover the hack when it rains?
- What kinds of mounting hardware is available for the hack?
- Will your dog fit into the hack?
- Do you want a windshield?
- Do you want a sidecar brake?
- How well do you want the look of the hack to match the motorcycle?
- Will the hack be used or new?
- What do the closest sidecar shops sell or recommend?
- If I sell the hack someday can I convert it back to human seating?

**Sidecar Mounts: Universal Mounts and Sub-frames**

Always have your sidecar mounted by a dealer or well-regarded experienced professional installer. Internet forums are filled with horror stories about what happens when "an experienced/expert friend" installed a sidecar for someone new to the sport.

If you are lucky the hack you purchase will have a mount specifically designed for the make and model motorcycle you plan to use to pull it. This is one of the big advantages of using a Harley Davidson sidecar on a Harley Davidson motorcycle.

After the dealer or professional sidecar installer has mated your sidecar to your motorcycle and test rides have confirmed it behaves and performs well you should mark all of the adjustment points with paint or nail polish so that if any slippage occurs you know how much and where. It should be an unusual event for a make/model specific mount, professionally installed, to slip out of adjustment as many of these are held in place by cotter pins. Just the same it is a cheap easy precaution to double check.

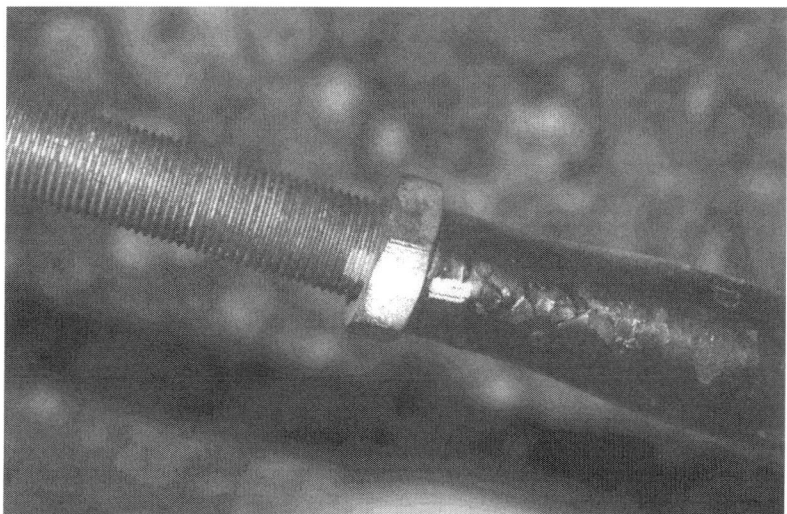

Once your sidecar is correctly adjusted, mark the adjustment points with paint so that you can inspect for slippage.

Some sidecar manufactures and vendors offer a "universal mount" and some even claim such mounts will "fit any motorcycle". Please be wary of such claims and research how successful these universal mounts have been for other customers.

A mount made to fit a very large variety of motorcycles likely has short-comings in some or all configurations when compared to make/model specific mounts.

In our experiences and the experiences of our friends, universal mounts are likely to come out of adjustment over time and require minor or major realignments.

If you end up using a universal mount it is very important to use paint or fingernail polish to mark the settings and positions of all of the points of the mount so that if any shifting or loosening happens you can detect and correct it right away. You should also perform regular checks on the entire system for stress and cracks. We recommend this for all mounts of course but in particular for universal mounts as they tend not to have the tried and true engineering history with all of the bugs worked out that you would find in a make/model specific setup.

**Custom Sub-frames**

What do you do if no make/model specific mounting system is made for your motorcycle and you don't want to use a universal mounting kit or no universal mounting it is available for your sidecar? The answer is that you can have a custom sub-frame fabricated by a sidecar shop that does metalworking and customization.

Custom sub-frames might not be much more expensive than a universal mount and they have the advantage of being optimized for your installation.

As we have recommended for many other topics, having this work done by a reputable shop is paramount. A reputable shop will design a sub-frame that is not only structurally reliable but will have the foresight to make sure the sub-frame does not have to be removed to leave good access to oil filters, cooling and oil lines or any other serviceable components.

A professionally made sub-frame will leave room for bike maintenance and access to important items like the VIN.

If you live in the mid-west USA, one of the best and most experienced sub-frame fabricators for BMW motorcycles is DBear Sidecar Works in Camden, Ohio.

**Popular Sidecars**

Producing a compendium of sidecars would be an amazing amount of work because so many manufacturers have come and gone over the approximately 100 years of the sport.

In the book we are going to cover a FEW of the more common and popular sidecar types available on the used or new market in the USA.

## B2 and BW classic BMW Hacks

As covered in previous chapters, much of sidecar history and design originated in Germany before and during the Second World War. One of the most common, utilitarian and durable sidecars of all time is the classic BMW 286/1. The classic BMW sidecar was produced primarily for the military's use. Once production ramped up the BMW 286/1 sidecar was produced by contractors such as Steib and variations were produced with slight changes in size such as the B2, BW38, BW40, BW42, BW43 etc.

These designs fell into the public domain and thousands have been produced in Germany, Russia and China. Today these are the standard sidecar bodies you will find on CJ750 and Ural motorcycles. They are often referred to as Steib sidecars but Steib never sold these to the public -- they only produced them under contract to BMW and later the German military, and they were not the only subcontractor.

The classic BMW sidecar has remained popular for over 75 years for good reason. It has excellent storage, a variety of configurations that allow for everything from gas cans, ammunition bins, machine gun mounts, windshields, ambulance stretchers and a spare wheel.

Ava, the chocolate lab shows her sidecar's bolt-on accessories.
(photo Mike Easton, used with permission)

From the dog rider's point of view this sidecar allows easy removal and installation of a seat for humans, is a good size for medium to large dogs, offers easy side access with a small step and step through. There is plenty of storage in the front and latching back trunk of the sidecar for nearly every dog accessory you could want with you. Covers are inexpensive and readily available to keep the sun and elements out when parked. The sidecar body is so sturdy you could almost say it was armored. The sheet metal body also makes it easy to attach a sturdy dog safety harness that can be operated from the motorcycle or far side of the sidecar.

If you want a sidecar for easy use by both dogs and humans this hack is a great choice. You can remove the bottom cushion of the classic BMW sidecar seat quickly leaving the back of the seat in place. A soft but easy to grip mat can be placed in the sidecar and now your dog has a well-padded and protected environment for riding.

A seat that can be easily added or removed allows use of the sidecar by both dogs and humans.

The principle limitation to this kind of sidecar is its size and weight. You will need a strong and reasonably large motorcycle to pull this sidecar, at least 750cc in most configurations. Not many interstate highway capable rigs use this sidecar, though it is not unheard of.

Although these sidecars were not originally designed with a sidecar brake, brakes are available from Ural and Chinese vendors.

## Steib Sidecars

Steib has been making sidecars almost as long as sidecars have been around.

Stieb at one time is claimed to have held 90% of the worldwide sidecar manufacturing market but ceased production in the 1960s as automobiles become the preferred family transportation in Europe.

A beautiful vintage Steib sidecar on a Zundapp motorcycle.

Reproduction Steib sidecars can be purchased through dealers in the USA and Europe along with all of the reproduction parts you could hope for.

Steib model numbers are easy to understand. The lineup starting with the LS 200, the smallest and lightest sidecar intended for 250cc bikes. It progresses up to the TR/S 500 for 500cc and larger motorcycles. The US vendor of Steib sidecars does not list an option for a sidecar wheel brake, however several websites do sell Steib wheel hubs that support a brake. Bench Mark Works, a vintage BMW restoration vendor, sells an improved suspension band that is more durable and reliable then the stock European reproduction suspension bands.

Because Steib sidecars are reproduction vintage sidecars they typically are installed on vintage motorcycles such as BMW, Zundapp, Royal Enfield or really anything retro or steampunk like vintage scooters.

From the dog rider's point of view the smaller Steib models are not easy for dogs to get in and out of without considerable modifications. If your dog is very agile he will be able to jump in but over time will likely scratch the fender's body paint and as he ages, he may risk being injured in the jump. The TR500 model, however, like the classic BMW BWXX series of sidecars has step through side access and a fender step, lots of storage and plenty of room.

## Velorex Sidecars

Velorex sidecars are probably the most well-known and common hacks produced today. Located in Czechoslovakia, Velorex (now Velorexport) is part of a manufacturing cooperative that started producing sidecars in cooperation with Jawa motorcycles in the 1970s.

The popularity of the lightweight low cost Velorex sidecars exceeded that of the Jawa motorcycles and while Jawa motorcycles are primarily sold in Europe, Velorex sidecars can be purchased worldwide from a large number of dealers.

The principle advantages of Velorex sidecars is that they are lightweight, inexpensive, common on the used marked, come in several styles and parts are readily available.

The 560 "family" of sidecars are the most common, with most of the sidecars sharing the same chassis and the variations being in the sidecar body. A larger 700 model is available that provides a great deal of storage and protection for the passenger from the wind and environmental elements. Nearly all models of the Velorex sidecars support an optional brake hub. Manuals and setup guides are freely available for download. Dealer support is generally regarded as very good with over 60 US dealers at the time of this writing.

Most Velorex sidecars have the option of installing a vinyl roof that can be used to operate the sidecar in inclement weather.

Velorex sidecars were originally designed to be attached to Jawa motorcycles and for other makes they offer a universal mount that according to the Velorex USA website "fits any motorcycle." We would recommend that you not take this at face value but consult an installer about using the universal mount on your motorcycle.

We found that the universal mount from Velorex was of very lightweight construction and after time would often lose its adjustments. We replaced the mounting hardware on all of our Velorex sidecars with custom sub-frames and found this greatly improved the handling of the rigs as well as removed the need for regular readjusting.

From a dog rider's point of view the usability of the Velorex sidecars vary with the models.

The chassis of all of the Velorex models mounts below the seat so to protect your dog's feet or belly when prone some kind of foam or soft protective well-secured cover will need to be made to cover the bolts and any sharp edges. Silicone glues with rubber sheet material can be used for this.

As of this writing four sidecar models are available from Velorex, the 562, 563, 565 and 700.

The 562/563 models are similar with styling that goes well with most bikes vintage and modern. For dogs these models will be difficult to get in and out of. To use these model sidecars, the dogs will need to be fairly agile and the owners will need to cover the fenders with a scratch resistant surface that offers a non-slippery foot hold. The seat will need to be entirely removed for medium sized dogs and some large dogs may have difficulty fitting without modification to the windshield or rear portion of the sidecar body.

Velorex 500-class sidecars are very popular.

An advantage that the 562/563 series have is that the windshield is easy to remove and customize. As discussed at the beginning of this chapter most dogs would prefer not to have a windshield and if they do have one will spend most of their time looking around the side of it.

The 562/563 sidecar windshield is a clear Plexiglas or Lexan sheet that is secured to at the bottom to the sidecar with a series of small bolts, a rubber liner to protect from stress and a metal band that attaches to a fiberglass lip.

Some dog owners simply remove the windshield as the look of the sidecar is not dramatically reduced, but for a nicer fit and finish you may consider having the windshield professionally cut down to a size low enough for your dog to look over, but that still provides a sporty look and some protection from the elements. However, if you cut down or change the shape of the stock windshield keep in mind the vinyl roof will no longer fit the sidecar.

The 565 model Velorex sidecar improves access for dogs jumping in and out of the sidecar with a partially hinged top and fender step.

The 562, 563 and 565 sidecars will all require removal of the seat and seat infrastructure for all but the smallest of dogs and unless you are highly creative, will not allow a quick and easy retrofit for human passengers.

The Velorex model 700 sidecar, like the 565 has a hinged top to help access into the sidecar, however because of the higher sidewall and reduced fender step in practice it is just as hard for a dog to enter and exit as the 562 and 563 models. The 700's windshield cannot be modified as it makes up part of the structure of the sidecar body.

The Velorex 700 sidecar provides weather protection and lots of storage.

Large dogs may have problems fitting into the 700 unless you remove the seatback which is not only makes the sidecar unsightly, but removes the locked storage area behind the seat, one of the 700's best features. The principle advantage to the 700 series for dog owners is the storage capacity and the protection from wind and elements. If you want a nearly enclosed sidecar that with a vinyl accessory can be made fully enclosed the 700 is a good choice.

Because the Velorex family of sidecars are light and small they work well for attachment to both small displacement motorcycles and higher performance interstate highway-going rigs.

**Other Sidecar Manufacturers**

There have been hundreds of different manufacturers of sidecars, some popular, some not and some went out of business while some continue on.

It is beyond the scope of this book to list all of the sidecar makes and models but if you know of some good compendiums please contact us and we will list them on the companion website for this book www.DogsRide.org.

**Riding at Night and Electrical System Issues**

As covered in Chapter 3, it is a very good idea to provide some lighting inside of the sidecar so that you can monitor your dog's situation during night riding.

Some sidecar designs, especially vintage rigs, have very poor lighting and visibility.

One inexpensive and easy remedy is to apply some black reflective tape to the back and sides of the sidecar. It sounds like an oxymoron but black reflective tape is a vinyl tape that appears dark black in daylight but at night becomes a bright white/tan reflector! This provides great nighttime visibility without sacrificing any vintage look.

As with most products you tend to get what you pay for so beware of cheap reflective tapes, we recommend 3M Scotchlite Reflective Striping Tape.
One drawback to riding vintage motorcycles at night is that many of them have 6-volt lighting systems that are borderline unsafe on modern roads at night. It is one thing for you to take a risk, but to risk the life and safety of your dog is even worse.

Now you don't see it, now you do. 3M black reflective tape provides night visibility without sacrificing daytime looks.

Many companies offer kits to convert 6-volt motorcycle electrical systems to 12-volt systems but these tend to be expensive and often require modifications owners do not want to do because they want to preserve the vintage configuration or look.

Several vendors are selling "super bright" 6-volt LED lighting systems that look vintage, do not require you to convert the bikes electrical system to 12-volt and provide impressively bright tail and brake lights.

12-volt LEDs on a plate bracket allow owners to keep the original 6-volt bulbs, electrical system and vintage looks while greatly reducing the chances of being rear-ended at night.

Another option is to buy bright 12-volt LED bulbs and use a $20 step up transformer. These solid state transformers will convert 1 to 1.5 amps of 6-volt power to 12 volts, enough to power plenty of super bright LEDs. The transformer is rugged and small enough to fit in most tail light housings. The advantage here is that it is less expensive than 6-volt super bright LEDs made specifically for motorcycle use and you don't have to convert your bike's entire electrical system. If you want to purchase some, search eBay for "Industry Grade DC 6v to DC 12v 1a Step-Up Converter".

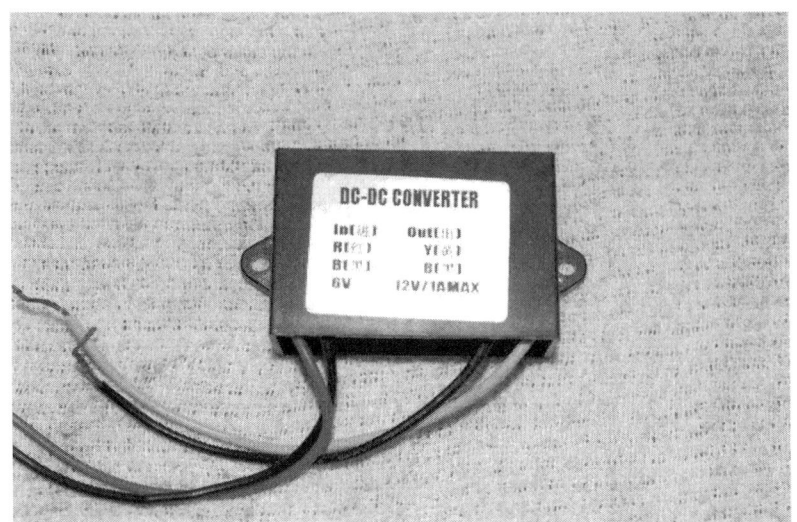

A 6 to 12-volt step-up transformer is an easy and inexpensive way to put super-bright LED lights on a vintage motorcycle.

# 7 DRIVER TRAINING

Would you advise a friend to learn to swim by reading a book? Perhaps not.

Likewise we don't advise learning to drive a sidecar rig by reading a book.

However, we can share some advice, tips, "gotchas," and recommendations.

To start with, if possible seek out a class on riding a motorcycle with a sidecar. Several classes take place around the U.S. each year and typically are announced in the United Sidecar Association's magazine or through social media.

If you are unable to attend a class, seek out experienced riders in your region for mentorship.

We don't advise self-training.

Tim went the self-teaching route and, although ultimately reasonably successful, he did experience several potentially life threating experiences. These could have been easily avoided had he taken a class or worked with a mentor.

Each sidecar rig is unique and should be test driven with proper weight in the sidecar by an experienced driver to assess the characteristics of the machine. These characteristics need to be noted by both the mentor and student.

The rig's characteristics and attributes should be recorded into a document that is kept with the bike for review, much like you would keep an owner's manual for a motorcycle listing the oil, plugs and maintenance requirements. The document should have all of the performance tendencies found while evaluating the rig under controlled circumstances as well as those found during ongoing riding and experiences by the owner.

## What to Expect When Riding a Sidecar Motorcycle

As explained in previous chapters each and every rig is unique in some way, most in many ways.

The most common challenges are the various circumstances in which a right-hand turn may bring the sidecar wheel up, and learning to deal with the rig pulling to the side when accelerating or decelerating.

Assuming the sidecar is on the right-hand side of the bike (some countries have the sidecar on the left-hand side), you will likely find that the turns toward the sidecar can be challenging and even dangerous under certain circumstances.

Even highly experienced riders must always use caution when making turns toward the sidecar in a lightly loaded rig or when breaking hard in a heavily loaded rig or worst of all braking during a steep hard turn.

Motorcyclists normally use leaning and counter steering to control the direction of their motorcycle. With a sidecar rig it is more like an ATV with the front forks doing the work of turning the vehicle.

Unlike an ATV the sidecar puts the center of gravity off to the side of the vehicle. This means that steering and breaking can cause the body of the rig to want to rotate around the center of gravity in a place that most people are not used to.

The center of gravity can change dramatically depending on the rig's setup, the weight in the rig and the weight on the motorcycle.

The key to learning, loving and safely piloting a sidecar is to have good situational awareness.

If you "wake up" from thinking about your daily troubles or inspirations during your ride and find yourself running fast into a turn, you don't have good situational awareness.

This does not mean you cannot sit back and enjoy the ride, but it does mean you need to apply enough attention to the road to be able to accurately forecast conditions at least 10 - 20 seconds into the future.

Turning, braking and general riding of a sidecar rig takes more situational awareness than a car or solo motorcycle. Driving a sidecar rig has more in common with piloting a boat or aircraft because your mind must always be "ahead of the vehicle."

## The Dreaded Right-hand Turns

The most famous place riders experience trouble is when turning toward the sidecar, which for most people in the U.S. is on the right side.

If a right-hand turn is made too aggressively the sidecar wheel can come up from the ground.

Several things happen at once under this condition. First the center of gravity now moves, changing the characteristics of the vehicle. Secondly, you are now on two wheels and are now driving a counter weighted motorcycle.

This condition can be easier to notice on first onset if your sidecar has a stiff suspension. A suspension that is light with more travel can mask the early sensations of the sidecar wheel leaving the ground.

Unless you have a very stout mule, performing this maneuver at speed with a passenger or loaded sidecar can damage the motorcycles wheels, spokes, swing arm, sub-frame and frame.

If this is an unplanned maneuver a more immediate concern could be unintended impact with other vehicles or objects.

To return the sidecar wheel to the ground simply undo the maneuver that got the wheel up. By reducing the degree of the right-hand turn, and perhaps slowing down, the rig should return to being a well-controlled three-wheeled vehicle.

If you are traveling slow enough and have left enough margin in the road to shallow your turn, this surprise will likely result in nothing more than you learning about the performance boundaries of your rig.

However, if you did not leave sufficient margin in the lane to the left of you, then you might find your corrective maneuver placing you in a dangerous situation.

The chances of entering into an inadvertent "wheel up maneuver" increase exponentially with speed, steepness of turn and reduced weight in the sidecar.

The chances of having accident or injury from an inadvertent "wheel up maneuver" are high if you did not leave some room to the left of the rig in your driving lane.

Avoiding inadvertent "wheel up maneuvers" is simple and straightforward. Always take right-hand turns SLOWER than you think you should, leave as much margin on the left of the rig as allowable under the circumstances and always maintain situational awareness.

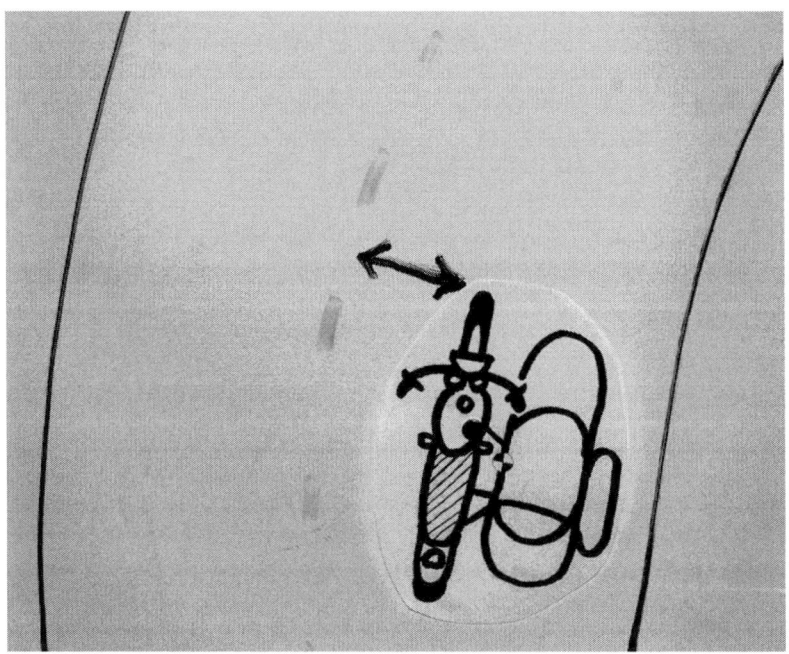

Always leave room in a turn.

## Turns on Hills

As previously mentioned, in a sidecar rig your center of gravity is likely to be found wondering around in strange places. This makes a sidecar rig's behavior when making turns on an up-hill or down-hill slope difficult to predict.

Even a small turn on a grade can put a rig's center of gravity near the tipping point where a wheel up is ready to progress.

**Look where you want to go and maintain situational awareness.**

Fear is the mind-killer. Practice turns under controlled conditions until you start looking forward to the challenge of a twisty-turny road, just like you did as your motorcycle skills evolved.

**TIP:** Many sharp turns will "tell you" the maximum speed to use a hundred feet before the beginning of the turn.

Do you know those little yellow speed signs below the "sharp turn" warning signs? Yes, those signs everyone one seems to ignore?! These are golden nuggets of knowledge to sidecar riders.

If you see a yellow and black turn sign with a small "speed" sign underneath (such as 25 MPH) that is the maximum speed at which you should take that corner in a sidecar rig, especially if it's a turn toward the sidecar.

**Hard Braking**

The second most likely area of concern to a new sidecar rider is understanding the possible outcomes of hard breaking.

A vehicle's center of gravity (CG) "wants" to be lined up with the breaking force applied by the tires to the road when you apply the brakes.

Center of Gravity Symbol

In a motorcycle the center of gravity (CG) is generally well aligned under most circumstances with the wheels. Therefore when you apply the brakes very hard the body of the motorcycle tends to want to continue to move in same direction it was moving before you applied the brakes.

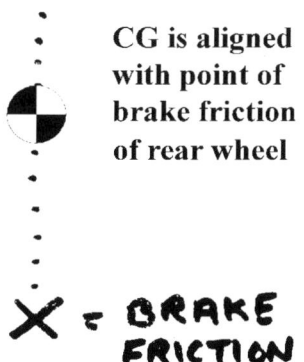

If the center of gravity is aligned with the rear wheel's point of braking friction no turning tendancy is expected

**CG is aligned with point of brake friction of rear wheel**

X = BRAKE FRICTION

Another way to think of this is if the center of gravity (CG) is aligned with the direction of movement, applying the rear brake will NOT cause a tendency of the bike to want to turn.

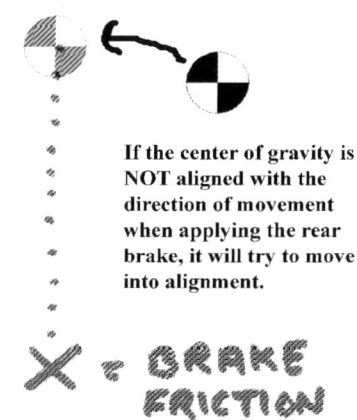

If the center of gravity is NOT aligned with the direction of movement when applying the rear brake, it will try to move into alignment.

X = BRAKE FRICTION

If the center of gravity (CG) is located to the side of the direction of movement, applying the rear brake will cause the CG to try to align with the direction of movement.

With a sidecar attached to a motorcycle the center of gravity (CG) has been moved toward the sidecar.

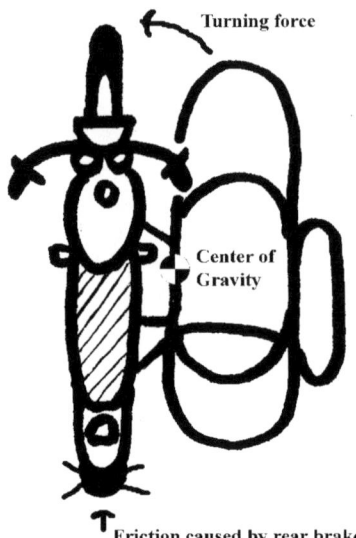

In a sidecar rig if you apply the rear brake the center of gravity (CG) will "want" to get in line with the braking force of the rear wheel.

You can think of this as meaning that the sidecar will want to be where the motorcycle is, thus producing a force that appears to the rider as if the rig wants to make a turn away from the sidecar (typically left).
Is the center of gravity explanation and graphics not working for you? Perhaps a less technical analogy would be better.

Let us imagine the effect in a new way. Let's say that we have two cardboard cut-outs. One of a motorcycle, another of a motorcycle with a side car.

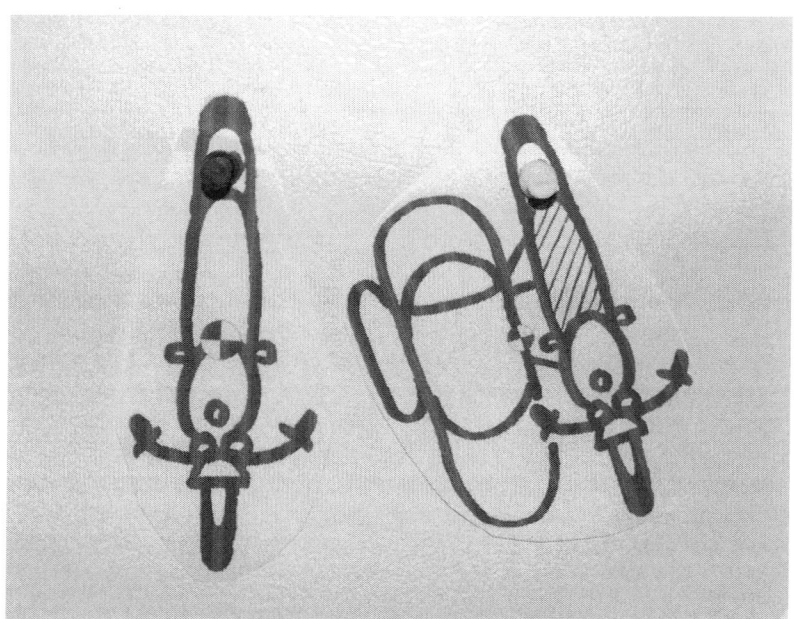

Using a push-pin on a drawing may help you visualize what happens when you use the rear brake only when driving a sidecar rig. Note that the CG moves to be under the push-pin.

Now imagine putting the cutouts on a board and inserting push-pins where the rear wheel of each motorcycle would be.

What happens?

Gravity causes the cutouts to balance their weight under the push-pins.

The motorcycle says in line, while the cutout of the sidecar rig swings with the side car butting in. From the perspective of an imaginary rider the cutout is trying to make a left-hand turn.

The extent to which the rider experiences this action depends on many factors but principally speed, amount of brake applied, and position of the CG. The more weight in the sidecar generally the greater the distance between the CG and the motorcycle.

In a sidecar rig if you apply the front brake only, the center of gravity (CG) will "want" to get in line with the braking force of the front wheel.

In this case the result could be a tip-over with the rear wheel leaving the ground and the nose of the sidecar hitting the ground.

The procedure for dealing with these issues is pretty straightforward. Try to avoid going too fast in the first place. Realize that hard braking is going to make the bike feel like it wants to make a turn away from the sidecar (left typically).

If you try to break during a right-hand turn the braking action will work against your turn. This limits how strongly you can apply the brakes in a challenging right-hand turn.

If you have left yourself no margin in a fast steep right-hand turn, applying a hard rear brake action might just force you out of your turn, sending you into an adjacent lane!

Improper braking can cause the rig to fight against your turn.

## Sidecar Wheel Brakes

Some sidecars can be outfitted with a brake on the sidecar wheel. This brake is sometimes actuated with the rear motorcycle brake or sometimes has a second independent brake pedal next to the rear brake pedal.

Having a sidecar wheel brake changes the playing field with the rig's CG. You can now apply the rear brakes without the CG "wanting" to cause the sidecar to induce a turn.

If you liked the push-pin analogy, having a sidecar brake is like having two push-pins, one stuck in the rear motorcycle wheel and the other stuck in the side car wheel. The cut-out now hangs straight down.

Dogs Ride. Motorcycle Sidecar Riding for Dogs (and Humans)

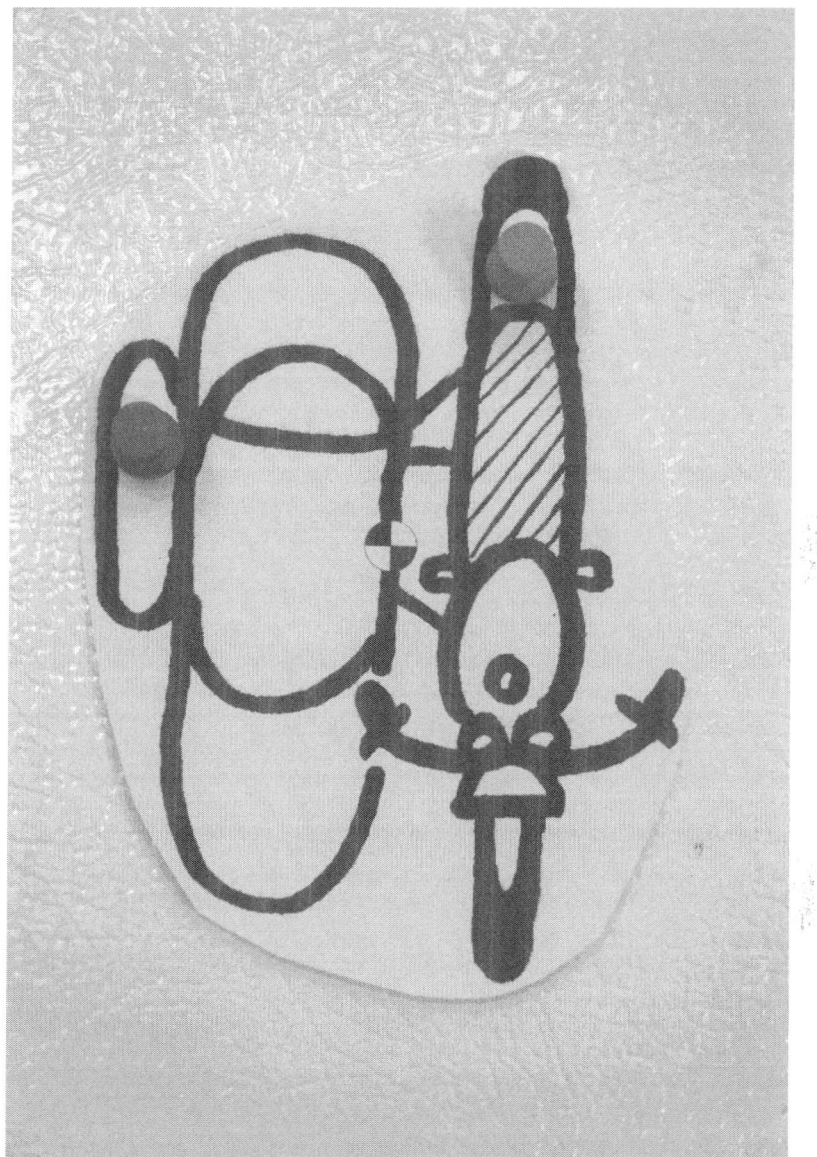

With a brake on the sidecar wheel the CG stays between the rear wheels and the turning tendency is removed.

If the sidecar brake can be actuated independently you can even use it to "assist" or induce a turn toward the side car (right-hand typically).

As previously mentioned hard braking in a right-hand turn can increase the challenge of a right-hand turn and perhaps put you in the lane of oncoming traffic.

By applying a sidecar-only brake you can apply the brake during a steep right-hand turn with less chance of bringing the side car wheel up off of the ground. Pretty cool huh?

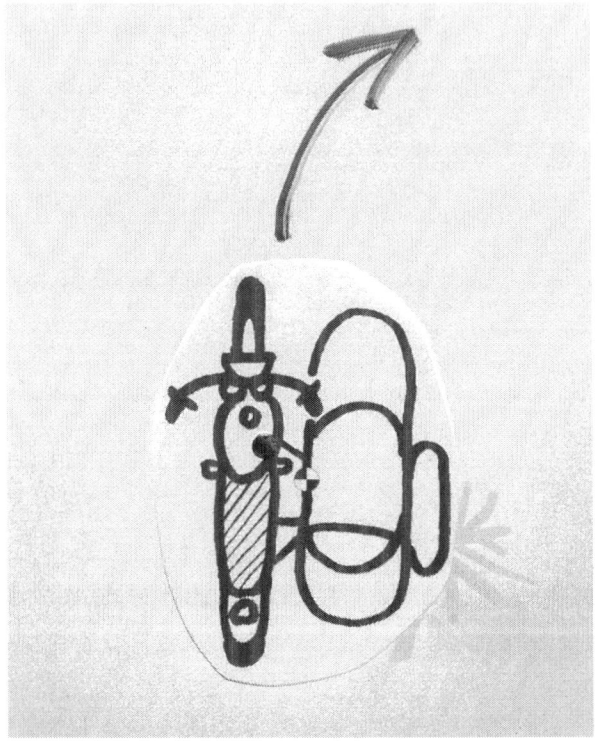

Using the sidecar brake only causes a right-hand turn tendency.

Should you have a sidecar brake installed?

We can't answer that question for you. We can say that most rigs do not have sidecar brakes installed but you should ask your mentor and sidecar installer about their opinion.

Many rig owners find the added expense and complexity of a sidecar brake is not worth the trouble as you still must maintain situational awareness when riding and judging turns and stops.

If you plan on riding a heavily loaded rig during adverse conditions the value of having a sidecar brake goes up.

## Reverse on a Motorcycle

To some people's astonishment many large touring motorcycles have a reverse gear.

Likewise, some sidecar rigs also have a reverse because it can be difficult to get off the rig and push it when you can't drive out of a parking spot.

If a reverse was not included in your rig, aftermarket electric systems can be added, like the units sold by Truma, TXP, 3Wheels.org, Powrtouch and Purpleline.

If you don't have or want a reverse on your rig you can learn some tips and tricks to make maneuvering out of forward blocked locations easier.

Choose parking spaces that have a slight uphill gradient. To back out of these spaces simply pull in the clutch give a small nudge to the ground with your foot and let the weight of the rig and gravity do the work for you.

Find parking spaces that you can drive through so that you are facing out when you park.

"All right, I screwed up and parked in such a way I have to get off of the rig to push it. What now?"

The rig can get heavy and be more difficult to control than you expect in these circumstances. Plus there could be unseen crazy parking lot drivers afoot. It is very important that you be able to stop the rig if it starts rolling in a way you do not wish it to, or if you are suddenly blocked.

To take control of this problem put the rig in first gear and check to make sure the ignition is turned off. This configuration allows you to use the clutch handle as a braking device. This is important because the front and back brake levers will be largely out of reach when you are off the rig pushing it.

The next advantage to using the clutch as a braking device is that the rig "fails brake on". If your hand slips off of the clutch handle the clutch engages and the bike stops. The last thing you want is a run-away rig and this can help prevent such a situation.

## The Good News

We hope that you have not been scared off by the "strange behavior" many sidecar rigs have.

We are confident that if you apply good judgment and practice the skills you have learned with your mentor(s) you will find sidecar rigs as safe and enjoyable as your motorcycle.

Sidecars do have some advantages over motorcycles; one of them is that they are much less likely to tip over on dirt, gravel, wet or icy roads. They don't have sidestands that will sink into hot asphalt and tip your bike over. They are not as sensitive as a motorcycle is to being parked on a hill.

Sidecars are also a great option for people that have problems riding a solo motorcycle because of lack of strength, balance issues or other challenges.

Left turns (away from the sidecar) are stable and very fun!

A dog outfitted sidecar makes a great grocery hauler!

**Getting on the Rig and Learning to Ride**

As previously mentioned, the ideal situation would be to do as little self-teaching as possible. Classes and mentors are extremely helpful.

If you have years of experience riding motorcycles, some of that experience may work against you, as often it's easier to learn a skill then to unlearn a skill.

Experienced motorcyclists and novices alike should, in addition to using classes and mentors, consult the resources chapter in this book to extend their knowledge of our sport.

One good but often overlooked resource is your state Division of Motor Vehicles. All 50 U.S. states publish a free, downloadable guide to motorcycling which includes special sections for sidecars and trikes.

Any specific equipment or licensing required by your state will be listed in these guides as well as good advice to operating sidecars on the state roads.

Here is how the DMV describes entering a turn to leave sufficient margin for a wheel up correction.

"Check opposing traffic carefully, and if safe, enter the curve toward the outside of your lane. This increases your line of sight through the curve and reduces the effective radius of the curve. As you turn, move toward the inside of the curve, and as you pass the center, move to the outside to exit, always remembering to stay in your lane"

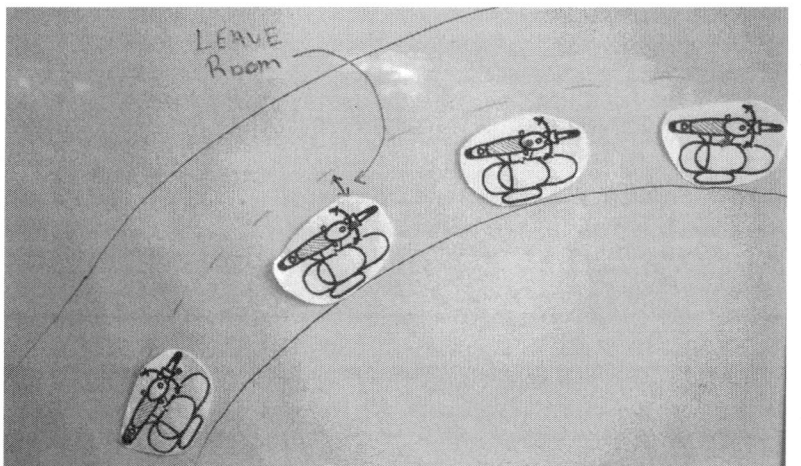

The DMV handbook gives a good recommendation on making turns with a sidecar rig. Enter the curve near the outside of the lane then stay near the inside during the turn.

When starting your practice it should be in a parking lot or other location free of other traffic.

Bring with you various weights that will NOT easily slide or shift in the sidecar. Sandbags such as those used for securing photographic equipment are inexpensive and ideal. Water jugs can also be used but while it is easy to reduce weight with these, adding weight can be more time consuming.

Don't use your dog as weight while practicing.

**"Flying The Chair"**

It is likely that one of the first practice maneuvers you will do in your class or with your mentor is called "Flying The Chair."

Flying the chair technique is done by purposefully lifting the sidecar into the air. It is a practice used by students and experts alike to learn and evaluate the performance of a rig in sharp turning conditions.

It is critical to remember that this is done with the sidecar EMPTY.

You may have seen videos of performers flying the chair with passengers but these rigs were likely reinforced for such performances or after the videos were taken the owners eventually discovered broken spokes and perhaps even damaged swing arms and frames.

Not all rigs can fly the chair without suffering damage. Some vintage designs like the CJ750 have such heavy sidecars that extended periods of flying the chair can result in broken rear wheel spokes.

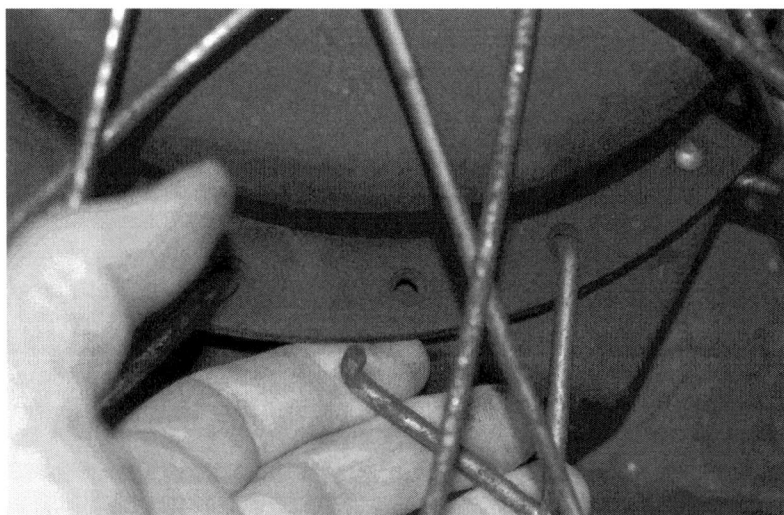

Flying the chair with too much weight in the sidecar may result in broken spokes or worse.

However, many rig designs, especially those with fiberglass or light sidecars can lift the sidecar for the periods of time used in training without serious consequences.

Having experience and practice under controlled conditions bringing up the sidecar wheel and recovering is absolutely invaluable.

Another likely training exercise your class or mentor will have to do is to run the rig in controlled circumstances with varying amounts of weight in the sidecar. With a range of various weights you will be asked to practice turns, hard braking and other riding combinations.

If successful, these and other training tools will give you the skills to identify when your sidecar wheel might leave the ground under a range of conditions, how to quickly stop your rig and bring confidence to your riding.

**Does this rig make my butt look big?**

Another common issue with learning to ride a sidecar rig, or riding a rig that is new to you, is judging the distance to the sidecar tire and fender without actually looking over while you are riding.

A good rider will almost never run the sidecar wheel up over a curb and will be able, when space is adequate, to dodge potholes in the road.

This ability will not come naturally and is of course typically unique to each rig.

There are many possible methods for learning this skill that your mentors may suggest. One such method is to place a sandbag in a parking lot and try to get your sidecar wheel as close as you can without hitting it. After mastering this, try other exercises such as getting as close with the INSIDE of the tire to the bag as you can or intentionally hitting (at slow speed) a serious of sandbags strategically placed around a course.

Knowing where the wheel is located does not mean you know how far the fender goes out. Therefore, once wheel position is mastered the next exercise is to miss soft traffic cones or other soft light items that will not damage your fender as you try to drive as close to them as you can.

**Passenger Management**

Specific issues related to dealing with dog situations in a sidecar were addressed in previous chapters. In this chapter we need to discuss passengers of the human kind.

NEVER take a passenger on the back of the motorcycle when the sidecar is empty.

Unless you have a heavy sidecar and a very heavy dog, you should not take a passenger on the back of the motorcycle when riding your dog in the sidecar.

If you feel that you have enough weight in the sidecar with your dog and other items that you can take a passenger on the back of your motorcycle, do so with extreme caution and realize that your CG will be in a location that you have never ridden with before.

Some rigs may have the passenger foot pegs removed or blocked by the sidecar mounting hardware. If this is the case it is not safe to take passengers behind the rider.

Like dog passengers, human passengers can be just as distracting and needy (no, really). Remember to DRIVE FIRST and react to passengers second. It does not matter what is happening to the passenger in the side car, crashing will not improve the situation.

Your first responsibly is to maintain your situational awareness and find a way to safely slow then stop the rig before reacting to a situation in the sidecar.

A passenger losing their cool over a spider crawling over their leg should not induce a traffic accident.

You may find out once reaching a stop at the side of the road that your passenger was simply wildly excited about a neighborhood lawn ornament or an old friend you just drove by. When the passenger exclaims "you did not have to pull over for that!" it will be a good time to explain to your passenger that flailing and screams of joy and excitement are indistinguishable from signs of panic.

When at speed, the rider has to keep eyes on the road ahead, wind will be in everyone's ears, and in this situation it will be difficult to discern the nature of excited happenings in the sidecar.

Communication systems such as ChatterBox radios can help with passenger management and increase the enjoyment of rides where wind noise makes communication difficult or impossible.

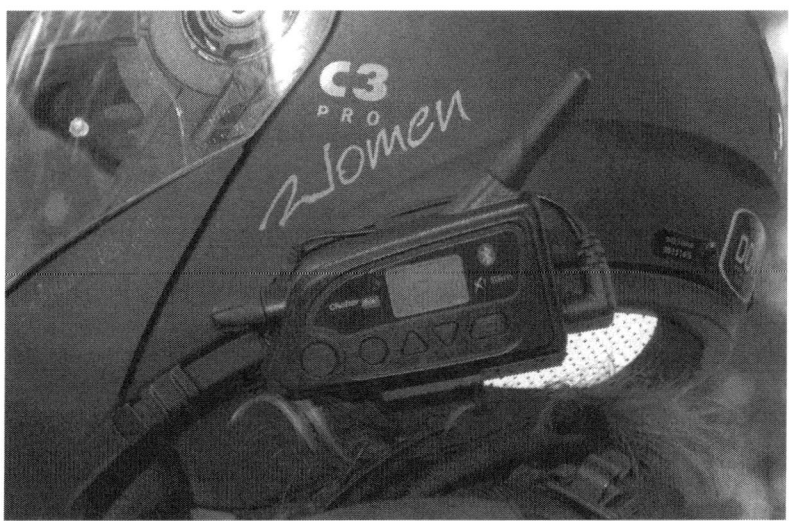

2-way motorcycle to motorcycle radios can also be used to communicate to human sidecar passengers, a trainer/mentor, or to other motorcycles on a group ride.

Working out a signal system with your human passengers before you ride, such as "tap me on the leg and give me a thumbs down if you have a problem" can go a long way in preventing incidents.

**I have learned to ride a sidecar rig! What now?**

This is time for congratulations but not for slacking off!

A good rider is always a learner and as you ride you will come across new experiences. Hopefully, you will learn from these new experiences.
Many seasoned riders will ride for hundreds of hours with a passenger then find themselves on a quick errand with an empty car and almost tip over the rig because they let their "muscle memory" overcome situational awareness.

After a winter or season of not riding you owe it to yourself but especially your passenger to put the weights in the sidecar and do some practice runs around the neighborhood. The "spring rustys" are serious business.

Periodically, run back through the exercises you learned in class or from your mentor, especially after a period of no riding.

# 8 EVENTS, GIVING BACK

You can put the attention your sidecar dog gets to good use by representing local dog rescue groups at parades and events.

With great power comes great responsibility and sidecar dogs are a powerful attractant.

Once you and your sidekick have become proficient on the roadways we suggest you see out opportunities to help the communities around you, especially those that serve the four-legged populace.

If you like this book please keep in mind that it is self-published so there is almost no marketing budget. Word-of-mouth is the principle means of promotion for this book. By reviewing and recommending this book on Amazon.com and social media we believe you will be aiding in helping this sport and the rescue dog community (a portion of the book proceeds are donated to rescue dogs and no-kill shelters).

Hercules d'Boxer visiting with some scouts.
(Handler JD "PupDaddy" Whitaker, used with permission)

Animal shelter fund raisers, motorcycle awareness events and even the town 4th of July parade can be an opportunity to share some of the wonderful experiences that come with having a sidecar riding dog companion.

If you go on a benefit ride hosted by a motorcycle club, keep in mind that you will be using the road somewhat differently than your solo motorcycle brethren. You might want to hang to the back of the pack or at least let them know you won't be taking the corners as fast as they do or making quick stops.

If you know of any good causes or events that dog sidecar riders could aid by participation let us know by email or posting it on the Facebook page for this book.

## A Dog Owner's Responsibilities

Because we love our dogs so very much, it's hard to imagine anyone not loving them as we do. Parents suffer from this same affliction when they fail to see how their adorable toddler's squeals of joy during a restaurant meal might not be appreciated by the people at the next booth or the waitress that has to clean up the food under the table.

Because we are sometimes blinded by our love., this is a good time for a reminder that taking your dog to public places is a privilege in this country, and one which some dog owners abuse. When dog owners ignore leash laws the result is often that dogs are banned from the premises. Dogs are banned from most national parks, most beaches, stores, apartment buildings, restaurants, and many outdoor events and running tracks. A few irresponsible owners ruin it for all of us when they allow their pets to run off leash, fail to clean up after them, allow them to bark incessantly, or allow them to approach other dogs and people without permission.

Someone gets bit, scared, muddy, or annoyed, and a new NO PETS sign goes up.

All dog owners have a responsibility to practice good dog owner etiquette to preserve the few privileges we still enjoy.

We do not recommend flexi-leashes because they get tangled around people and other dogs, and they allow the dog to lead you, rather than the other way around. Teach your dog to respectfully walk by your side. A 6' leash is plenty long for what a dog needs to do in public. If you need to pull him back to you in a hurry (such as because there is another dog barreling toward you and a fight looks eminent) you need instant control.

- You must clean up after your dog …and carry the bag to the nearest garbage can.
- Leash aggression is common….never allow your dog to sniff another dog without the owner's permission, and move aside or put yourself between your dog and other dogs when passing on trails or sidewalks.
- Two dogs should be introduced by walking them side by side, not directly face to face.
- Not everyone loves dogs ….don't allow your dog to approach people without their invitation.
- Likewise, use every opportunity to instruct children (and adults) to NEVER approach a dog without its owner's permission, and thank them when they ask.
- NEVER kiss or put your face near a strange dog's face, no matter how friendly the owner claims the dog to be.

Many dog owners feel the same way about their dogs as others do about their children: they are part of the family. But dogs must mind their manners too: owners should ensure that dogs do not jump on, brush against, or frighten other people. When two dogs pass, both owners should realize that many dogs don't like to meet face-to-face and this scenario should be avoided. If each owner keeps their dog on their left, the owners will be passing face to face, not the dogs.

Obedience and structure is very much appreciated by dogs, who are descended from wolves and are inherently in need of a strong pack leader. If your dog does not respect and trust you to provide consistent structure and clear expectations, he may become anxious and fearful or take it upon himself to make the decisions that you are clearly not able to make. Don't put the dog in this position. Give him the assurance that in your calm strong presence, the dog has nothing to fear and no decisions to make other than following your lead.

Like well-behaved children, dogs should be seen but not heard when adults are trying to have a conversation. Your dog should be able to lie quietly and calmly while you enjoy a meal or a conversation. No pulling, pacing, jumping, whining --- just calm attentiveness. The more you take your dog in public and practice the rules, the calmer he will be. A well trained dog is a wonderful companion – so put the work into it and help us give dogs and dog owners a good reputation.

**Rescue Dogs**

Petey won the rescue dog lottery when he met up with sidecar driver Tom Wells. (photo used with permission)

Every dog in a shelter is waiting for someone to discover its hidden gifts and talents. If given the chance through attention, training, leadership, consistency, and understanding the mind of a dog, any dog can shine.
There are so many dogs begging for someone to give them a chance; here are some things that people can do:

Foster a dog for a rescue group until a permanent home can be found. Get to know the dog's strengths so you can help find the perfect home for him or her.

Take the time to train and socialize your dog well – don't be one of those people who gives up on a dog because of annoying behavior that could have been solved with some effort in training, or because you never gave your dog the chance to show you who he could be.

Don't buy a purebred puppy – there are wonderful dogs of all ages waiting at shelters across the country. But if you must buy a purebred, also donate to rescue groups and shelters to give less fortunate dogs a chance.

Tell the world when you've helped a dog in need …that's one of the reasons going to events with our dogs is so important to us. One of our dogs, Bourbon, is a poster dog for what can be accomplished when you don't give up on a dog. Every dog, like every person, is elevated by the love and respect shown toward it, and by the way in which its talents are recognized and received.

Rescue dog Archie and Tom Wells attending an event riding a Harley Davidson and a Liberty sidecar (photo used with permission)

# 9 RESOURCES

**Official Book Companion Media**

We hope to add value to the mission of this book by donating a portion of the proceeds to local no-kill shelters and rescue dogs.

Additionally, we would like to provide supplemental information that did not get into the book as well as share ongoing events through internet resources.

Any hints, tips, products or events that you would like to submit to us are very welcome and we will do our best to share them with sidecar dog fans everywhere.

The official book web page is: www.DogsRide.org

The official book Facebook Page is:
https://www.facebook.com/DogsRide.Org

We can also be reached through email at: bmwcyclist@yahoo.com

**Sidecars and Dogs**

**Sit Stay Ride.** A fantastic documentary about sidecar dogs and their owners. This professional independent film production is another must for anyone even remotely interested in the topic.

www.sidecardogs.com

**Freedom on Both Ends of the Leash.**

An adventure riding book and journal media series.

Born in 1948 in France, a full blooded Armenian, he moved to the United States in his mid-twenties and worked successfully as a Five Star Chef around the country. His only child Lance passed away from liver cancer. Leaving it all behind, with his sweet rescued pit-bull buddy "Spirit", and a motorcycle with a sidecar, they left for the road camping full time, writing a journal and climbing the ladder of this School of Life. They are still on the road. You cannot miss them!

Learn more here:
www.FreedomOnBothEndsOfTheLeash.com
www.TheOasisOfMySoul.com

**Sidecar Resources**

*The Sidecarist* **magazine.** The magazine of the United Sidecar Association. A must-have publication with articles, advertisements and other resources. This magazine is included with membership in the USCA and they also have a wonderful website with forum and Facebook page.

http://www.sidecar.com/

**Sidecar Operator's Manual 2003** - By Hal Kendall
A free download found on several internet sites. A very compressive book on the history, use and setup of sidecars.

**Proficient Motorcycling** (series) by David Hough. David Hough has written several award-winning books on motorcycling techniques, most with sections on sidecars. *Driving a Sidecar Outfit* is available for download for $35.

**Bench Mark Works**, BMW parts, service, Steib Sidecars and a number of improvements for operating older bikes and sidecars on modern roads. www.BenchMarkWorks.com

**DMV Manuals.** We strongly recommend reading the motorcycle drivers manual for your state for good advice and an understanding of the laws that govern sidecar use. http://www.dmv.org/manuals.php

**Dog Training Resources:**

**All About Dogs Training Academy**, John Smith, 4008 Holbrook Ave. Cincinnati, OH 45226 (www.allaboutdogsohio.com)

*The Thinking Dog – Crossover to Clicker Training* by Gail Tamases Fisher, Dogwise Publishing, Washington, U.S.A. 2009

*Don't Shoot the Dog* by Karen Pryor, Bantam Books 1999

*How to be the Leader of the Pack and Have Your Dog Love You for it!* by Patricia MCConnell, PhD. MCConnell Publishing, Ltd. Black Earth, WI. 1996

*The Other End of the Leash: Why We Do What We Do Around Dogs.* By Patricia McConnell, Ballantine Books, NY 2002

*How to Be Your Dog's Best Friend: The Classic Training Manual For Dog Owners* by the Monks of New Skete, 2002

**Product Recommendations:**

KONG® Comfort Dog Harness & Traffic Loop

Ruffwear Climate Changer Dog Coat.

Randakk Cycles's spin-on oil filter adapter and oil cooler kit.

Chef's Comfort Mat 18" x 30" from BigLots ™ or Amazon.com for use in outfitting sidecar for dog use. Faux-leather foam filled comfort mat, Anti-fatigue, non-toxic, non-slip, mildew resistant, easy to clean, waterproof. Available in a number of colors.

Rio Beach Total Sun Block Umbrella. Great clamp-on umbrella to keep the side car cool.

**Other Resources:**

Dogs Ride. Motorcycle Sidecar Riding for Dogs (and Humans)

**Barrington Motor Works**, Vintage BMW Motorcycle Restoration. The ultimate guide to 1955-1970 BMW twin motorcycles and sidecars.

**AMA Mid-Ohio Vintage Motorcycle Days**. North America's largest motorcycle swap meet.

**Classic Motorworks (newsletters)**
http://www.cyclesidecar.com/

**La Quinita,** Dog friendly hotel chain. Indispensable when traveling.

**Dale Hollow**, Hendricks Marina allows dogs on certain houseboat rentals.

## 10 CREDITS, SOURCES

All photos taken by Tim O'Connor except as noted. All photos used with permission.

Front Cover: Cincinnati Street Style, Shay Nartker and Zach Napier. Used with permission.
See also: http://cincinnatistreetstyle.com/features/bourbon-bmws

Dan of DBear Sidecar Works, Camden Ohio for getting us on the right track with sidecars and keeping us on the road.

Kevin Johnson, North American Zundapp Rally host was very helpful in providing background information about Zundapp motorcycles.

Darlene and Sandy Wood for having the patience to help us make Bourbon the loving companion and superstar that he is.

Kevin Combs, a walking motorcycle Wikipedia who can sniff out a great bike better than a hound can find bacon.

Rick Markle, field repair mage and resurrector of the China Girl.

John C. Smith, The trainer who changed Bourbons life (and ours).

Sheltered Paws Animal Rescue, Tracey Staubach and others, saved Bourbon's life.

Dogs Ride. Motorcycle Sidecar Riding for Dogs (and Humans)

Floyd, our Mid-Ohio Vintage Days motorcycle mentor.

**Extra information about select photos:**

Photo of Steib Sidecar by Tim O'Connor, rig: 1953 Zundapp KS601 with Steib sidecar owned by Mike Mitchell speedwell, Tennessee.

Hercules d'Boxer's info:
JD "PupDaddy" Whitaker American Legion/Tour of Honor Rider Handler for Hercules d'Boxer 1977 BMW/Ural Custom Cafe 110k on bike - 50k on dog Riding in support of Darkhorse Lodge

Photo of Jeff Opsatnik's rear differential by Tim O'Connor; 70/30 -- first 2 wheel drive motorcycle, first motorcycle with hydraulic brakes. First bike with reverse. Germany's "JEEP" Zundapp KS750 --the ks750 ALWAYS was produced with a sidecar.

# ABOUT THE AUTHORS

Connie O'Connor has been riding motorcycles since she was a seven years old. With over 30 years of experience, she has ridden in all kinds of weather on many kinds of bikes. She has a sport pilot certificate and enjoys flying her light sport fixed wing aircraft. Connie has lived with dogs her entire life and is very dedicated to dog rescue and training. Connie is a biologist and her "real job" is to teach the public about science and the outdoors at a private non-profit nature center in Cincinnati.

Timothy O'Connor, husband to Connie O'Connor has made a living for the past twenty years in computer networking, security and technical training. Tim holds some of the highest certifications in the computer training industry and is a certified flight instructor. Tim holds numerous pilot ratings including Advanced Ground Instructor, Commercial Rotorcraft pilot, and FAA Fast Team Safety Volunteer. In addition to technical training and consulting, Tim co-hosted a top-rated radio show for three years on WNOP and has written cover and feature articles for such publications as ROTORCRAFT, EAA Sport Pilot, Sport Aviation, The Experimenter, Light Plane World, Homebuilt Rotorcraft, Powered Sport Flying, The Utopian and has published content in AVWeb, Technology First, jp4 and other publications.

Tim has been riding and restoring motorcycles since he was 13 years old.

Tim and Connie have been married for 7 years as June 2014.

Printed in Great Britain
by Amazon